SOFTWARE PRODUCT LINE – ADVANCED TOPIC

Edited by **Abdelrahman Osman Elfaki**

Software Product Line – Advanced Topic
Edited by Abdelrahman Osman Elfaki

Published by InTech

Janeza Trdine 9, 51000 Rijeka, Croatia

Publishing Process Manager Ana Pantar

Technical Editor Teodora Smiljanic

Cover Designer InTech Design Team

Additional hard copies can be obtained from orders@intechopen.com

Software Product Line – Advanced Topic, Edited by Abdelrahman Osman Elfaki
p. cm.
ISBN 978-953-51-0436-0

For EU product safety concerns:
IN TECH d.o.o., Prolaz Marije Krucifikse Kozulić 3, 51000 Rijeka, Croatia,
info@intechopen.com or visit our website at intechopen.com.

Meet the editor

Dr Abdelrahman Osman Elfaki is currently a senior lecturer at Management and Science University in Malaysia. He is involved in many projects and research related to software engineering in different countries, which refined his software engineering experience in both practical and academic fields. His current interests are modelling software product lines engineering and managing variability. He has published many papers related to his current interest.

Contents

Preface

Nowadays, Software Product Line (SPL) is considered to be one of the most popular technical paradigms and emerging methodologies in developing software products. The SPL consists of two main processes: the domain-engineering process and the application-engineering process. Collecting software assets regarding a specific business area falls within the domain-engineering process. The process of presenting software assets (in domain- engineering) is called variability modelling. The principal objective of application-engineering is to configure a successful specific software product from the domain-engineering process by managing SPL assets using variability modelling technique.

Modelling software assets in the domain-engineering is a substantial process as it identifies the commonality and variability within the domain-engineering process. Basically, the success of an SPL is largely dependent on effective variability management. Variability management refers to: 1) how variability is modelled, i.e., the representation of common features, uncommon features, dependency relations between features (require and exclude), and structure of the features in the form of parent and child features or formatted as variation points and variants; and 2) how to configure a valid software product, i.e., select some features or variants based on the configuration preferences in compliance with the variability-model rules.

Variability modelling techniques have been developed to assist engineers in dealing with the complications of variability management. The principal goal of modelling variability techniques is to configure a successful software product by managing variability in domain engineering. In other words, a good method for modelling variability is a prerequisite for a successful SPL.

On the other hand, the analysis of SPL aids the extraction of useful information from the SPL and provides a control and planning strategy mechanism for engineers or experts. In addition, the analysis of SPL provides a clear view for users. Moreover, its analysis ensures the correctness of the SPL. This book discusses these two issues: modelling and analysis of the SPL.

In the first part, modelling the SPL, Cavalcanti et al. introduce a new metamodel which integrates the processes of the SPL lifecycle. In addition, Cavalcanti's metamodel can be used as a communication tool between SPL developers and stakeholders. A real case study is used to validate the proposed metamodel. In the second chapter, Abd Halim et al. propose an approach for standardizing the representation of requirements and architectures in the SPL. Abd Halim's approach deals with the challenge of mapping the requirement models to architecture in domain-engineering. Abd Halim's chapter highlights and addresses requirement engineering issues in the SPL. Their approach is also corroborated by a real case study. In chapter three, Fouda Ndjodo and Ngoumou propose variability modelling approach dealing with business application. In their work, domain-engineering consists of business processes. This proposed technique addresses the challenges of adaptation, integration, conflict, and evolving of and between business processes. As a conclusion, this chapter deals with and solves critical issues in enterprise-systems SPL.

In the second part, analysis of the SPL, Tawhid and Petriu suggest a method for integrating performance analysis in the SPL. Their method uses the standard performance analysis technique to analyze the software product, so the challenge is how to apply the same technique for the SPL, since the SPL consists of group of products. A detailed example is provided to explain the method. Salinesi and Mazo introduce a method for detecting defects in the SPL. Their method discusses three criteria for verification: expressiveness, error-free, and redundancy-free. Some experiments have been done to validate the method and the computational scalability test has been performed to prove its applicability.

Dr. Abdelrahman Osman Elfaki
Management and Science University,
Malaysia

Part 1

Modelling

1

Handling Variability and Traceability over SPL Disciplines

Yguaratã Cerqueira Cavalcanti[1], Ivan do Carmo Machado[2], Paulo Anselmo da Mota Silveira Neto[1] and Luanna Lopes Lobato[1]
[1]*Federal University of Pernambuco, Reuse in Software Engineering – RiSE*
[2]*Federal University of Bahia, Reuse in Software Engineering – RiSE*
Brazil

1. Introduction

SPL has proven to be a successful approach in many business environments (Clements & Northrop, 2001a; Pohl et al., 2005a). Nevertheless, the SPL advantages do not come for free. They demand mature software engineering, planning and reuse, adequate practices of management and development, and also the ability to deal with organizational issues and architectural complexity. If these points are not considered, the product line success could be missed (Birk & Heller, 2007). Therefore, the development should be supported by auxiliar methods and tools, specially due to the complexity of the software systems that a SPL is supposed to deal with, represented by the variabilities.

Modeling can be used as a support mechanism to define and represent the variability involved in a SPL in a controlled and traceable way, as well as the mappings among the elements that compose a SPL. Many SPL projects are developed and maintained using model-based approaches (Dhungana et al., 2010). In this context, this chapter[1] proposes a metamodel representing the interactions among the assets of a SPL, developed in order to provide a way of managing traceability and variability. The proposed metamodel consists of representing diverse reusable assets involved in a SPL project, ranging from scoping to test artifacts, and also documentation.

The motivation to build the metamodel emerged from the experience gained during an industrial SPL project development that we have been involved in. This project consists of introducing SPL practices in a company working in the healthcare management systems domain, placed in Salvador, Brazil. The company currently has a single software development process and develops four different products: *SmartHealth*, a product composed by 35 modules (or sub-domains), which has the capability of managing a whole hospital, including all areas, ranging from financial management to issues related to patient's control; *SmartClin*, composed by 28 modules, is responsible to perform the clinical management, supporting activities related to medical exams, diagnostics and so on; *SmartLab* is a product composed by 28 modules, which integrates a set of features to manage labs of clinical pathology; all

[1] This chapter is an extension of our previous work published in VaMoS'11 conference (Cavalcanti et al., 2011)

these are desktop-based products, the only web-based product is the *SmartDoctor*, which is composed by 11 modules, and is responsible to manage the tasks and routines of a doctor's office.

Throughout this project, during the *scoping phase* (John & Eisenbarth, 2009) of the SPL life cycle, eight hundred and forty features (840) were consolidated. According to the time recorded in the management tool used in the project, dotProject[2], the scoping phase took approximately 740 man/hours of work. After this phase, *requirements engineering* started and the challenge faced during this phase was how to trace the variability and evolution among several assets such as product map (Clements & Northrop, 2001a), sub-domain documentation, features documentation, besides requirements, use cases, test cases and all the relationships among these assets. Although this work could be done with conventional tools, such as text and spreadsheet processors, it might be very error prone and not efficient. To understand such difficulties, consider the scenario where features should be retrieved from the existing products and then integrated with the products' requirements; afterwards, use cases must be linked to requirements, test cases linked to use cases, and so on. Clearly that would be not trivial to be performed with conventional tools.

Although diverse metamodels have been proposed in the literature (Anquetil et al., 2010; Bachmann et al., 2003; Bayer & Widen, 2001; Bühne et al., 2005; Moon et al., 2007; Sinnema et al., 2004; Streitferdt, 2001) in order to address variability and traceability aspects, they generally cover the SPL phases partially or do not treat such issues together through all the SPL disciplines. In this paper, we propose a metamodel which provides support for several SPL aspects, such as scoping, requirements, tests, and project and risk management. Furthermore, the metamodel was built upon a set of requirements concerning different issues identified in the literature, which is further discussed in Section 4. It also serves as a basis to understand the mappings among the SPL assets, communicate them to the stakeholders, facilitate the evolution and maintenance of the SPL, as well as it can be adapted to other contexts.

The remainder of this chapter is structured as follows: Section 2 presents an overview regarding SPL and its main concepts; Section 3 introduces the traceability conept; Section 4 specifies the requirements for a SPL metamodel; Section 5 describes the actual proposed metamodel, detailing its building blocks; in Section 6 an initial validation of the proposal is presented; Section 7 presents the related work; and finally, Section 8 concludes this work and outlines future work.

2. SPL essential activities

Software Product Lines combine three essential and highly iterative activities that blend business practices and technology. Firstly, the *Core Asset Development (CAD)* activity that does not directly aim at developing a product, but rather aims to develop assets to be further reused in other activities. Secondly, *Product Development (PD)* activity which takes advantage of existing, reusable assets. Finally, *Management* activity, which includes technical and organizational management (Linden et al., 2007). Figure 1 illustrates this triad of essential activities.

[2] **dotProject** is an open source, web-based project management application, and was used in the project reported in this work.

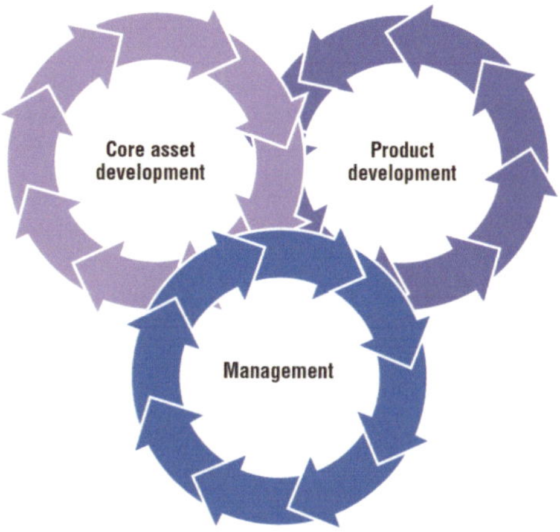

Fig. 1. Essential product line activities (Northrop, 2002).

2.1 Core Asset Development

Core Asset Development is the life-cycle that results in the common assets that in conjunction compose the product line's platform (Linden et al., 2007). The key goals of this activity are (Pohl et al., 2005b):

- Define variability and commonality of the software product line;
- Determine the set of product line planned members (scope); and
- Specify and develop reusable artifacts that accomplish the desired variability and further instantiated to derive product line members.

This activity (Figure 2) is iterative, and its inputs and outputs affect each other. This context influences the way in which the core assets are produced. The set of inputs needed to accomplish this activity are following described (Northrop, 2002). *Product constraints* commonalities and variations among the members that will constitute the product line, including their behavioral features; *Production constraints* commercial, military, or company-specific standards and requirements that apply to the products in the product line; *Styles, patterns, and frameworks* relevant architectural building blocks that architects can apply during architecture definition toward meeting the product and production constraints; *Production strategy* the whole approach for realizing the core assets, it can be performed starting with a set of core assets and deriving products (top down), starting from a set of products and generalizing their components in order to produce product line assets (bottom up) or both ways; *Inventory of preexisting assets* software and organizational assets (architecture pieces, components, libraries, frameworks and so on) available at the outset of the product line effort that can be included in the asset base.

Based on previous information (inputs), this activity is subdivided in five disciplines: *(i)* domain requirements, *(ii)* domain design, *(iii)* domain realization (implementation), *(iv)* domain testing and *(v)* evolution management, all of them administered by the management activity (Pohl et al., 2005b). These disciplines are responsible for creating the core assets, as well as, the following outputs (Figure 2) (Clements & Northrop, 2001b): *Product line scope* the description of the products derived from the product line or that the product line is capable of

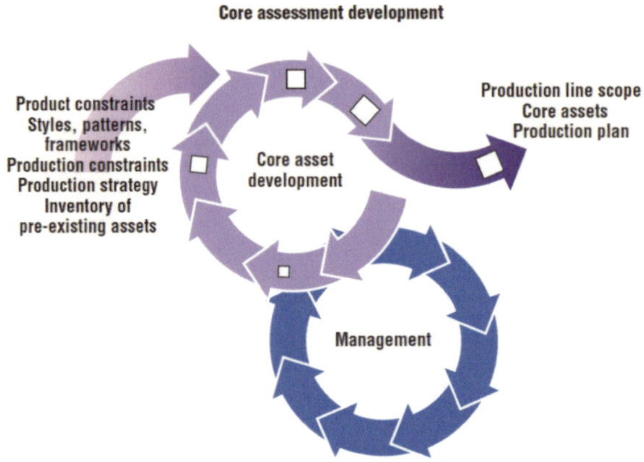

Fig. 2. Core Asset Development (Northrop, 2002).

including. The scope should be small enough to accommodate future growth and big enough to accommodate the variability. *Core assets* comprehend the basis for production of products in the product line, besides the reference architecture, that will satisfy the needs of the product line by admitting a set of variation points required to support the spectrum of products, theses assets can also be components and their documentation. The *Production plan* describes how the products are produced from core assets, it also describe how specific tools are to be applied in order to use, tailor and evolve the core assets.

2.2 Product development

The product development main goal is to create individual (customized) products by reusing the core assets previously developed. The CAD outputs (product line scope, core assets and production plan), in conjunction with the requirements for individual products are the main inputs for PD activity (Figure 3).

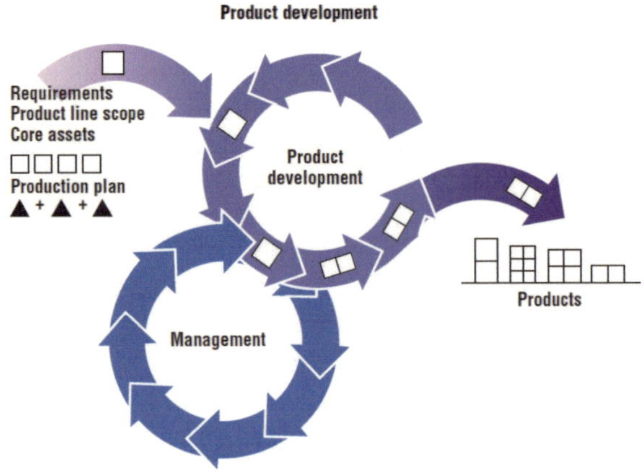

Fig. 3. Product Development (Northrop, 2002).

In possession of the production plan, which details how the core assets will be used in order to build a product, the software engineer can assemble the product line members. The product requirement is also important to realize a product. Product engineers have also the responsibility to provide feedback on any problem or deficiency encountered in the core assets. It is crucial to avoid the product line decay and keep the core asset base healthy.

2.3 Management

The management of both technical and organizational levels are extremely important to the software product line effort. The former supervise the CAD and PD activities by certifying that both groups that build core assets and products are engaged in the activities and to follow the process, the latter must make sure that the organizational units receive the right and enough resources. It is, many times, responsible for the production strategy and the success or failure of the product line.

2.4 SPL variability management

During Core Asset Development, variability is introduced in all domain engineering artifacts (requirements, architecture, components, test cases, etc.). It is exploited during Product Development to derive applications tailored to the specific needs of different customers.

According to Svahnberg et al. (2005), variability is defined as *"the ability of a software system or artifact to be efficiently extended, changed, customized or configured for use in a particular context"*. It is described through variation points and variants. While, the variation point is the representation of a variability subject (variable item of the real world or a variable property of such an item) within the core assets, enriched by contextual information; the variant is the representation of the variability object (a particular instance of a variability subject) within the core assets (Pohl et al., 2005b).

The variability management involve issues, such as: variability identification and representation, variability binding and control (de Oliveira et al., 2005). Three questions are helpful to variability identification, *what vary* the variability subject, *why does it vary* the drivers of the variability need, such as stakeholder needs, technical reasons, market pressures, etc. The later, *how does it vary* the possibilities of variation, also known as variability objects.

The variability binding indicates the lifecycle milestone that the variants related with a variation point will be realized. The different binding times (e.g.: link, execution, post-execution and compile time) involves different mechanisms (e.g.: inheritance, parameterization, conditional compilation) and are appropriate for different variability implementation schemes. The different mechanisms result in different types of defects, test strategies, and test processes (McGregor et al., 2004).

Finally, the purpose of variability control is to defining the relationship between artifacts in order to control variabilities.

3. SPL traceability

It most organizations and projects with mature software development processes, software artifacts created during the application of these processes end up being disconnected from each other. There are several factors leading to the lack of traceability among artifacts, as stated by Rilling et al. (2007). They are: (i) these artifacts may be written in different languages (natural language vs. programming language); (ii) the system is described by considering various abstraction levels/views (scoping and requirements vs. design or implementation); (iii) software processes do not consider maintenance of existing traceability links as a "must have" practice; and also (iv) there is a lack of adequate tool support to create and maintain traceability among software artifacts.

The lack of traceability among artifacts can be considered a major challenge for many software maintenance activities (Rilling et al., 2007). As a result, during the comprehension of existing software systems, software engineers are likely to spend an enormous effort on synthesizing and integrating information from various sources to establish links among these artifacts.

Indeed, by establishing traceability, engineers have the opportunity to understand how software artifacts interact with each other, in terms of relations and dependencies. Traceability links are indeed helpful when considering the evolutionary characteristic of the software artifacts, that are likely to be changed during its lifecycle.

According to Anquetil et al. (2010), establishing traceability yield a series of benefits, such as: (i) to relate software artifacts and corresponding design decisions, (ii) to give feedback to architects and designers about the current state of the development, allowing them to reconsider alternative design decisions, and to track and understand errors, and (iii) to ease communication between stakeholders, among others.

In SPL, where assets can be used by many products, traceability is even more important. A change in an artifact in a product line may lead to resultant changes in all products developed reusing such an artifact. Hence, it is necessary to define dependency relationships between the relevant artifacts to support consistent change integration (Moon et al., 2007).

Traceability practices vary widely-from high-end to low-end (Ramesh & Jarke, 2001). The prior use customized traceability knowledge for managing variability. Project managers may select traceability practices based on project characteristics such as system complexity, product line vs. single system software development, and degree of variety involved. The later take more of a "one-size fits all" approach to documenting traceability knowledge, and create simple traceability links between customer requirements, design, and code modules. While high-end practices aim at customer satisfaction and system quality, low-end are used just to meet organizational or customer-mandated quality requirements (Mohan & Ramesh, 2007).

4. Requirements for the SPL metamodel

We identified some work (Bayer & Widen, 2001; Bühne et al., 2005; Sinnema et al., 2004; von Knethen & Paech, 2002) that elicited different requirements which a metamodel for SPL should be in conformance with, in order to support properly the SPL development characteristics. The requirements are following described.

In (Sinnema et al., 2004), the authors propose four (4) requirements that a framework for modeling variability in SPL should have to support product derivation. However, the product derivation phase in SPL depends on how properly the previous phases are done. Therefore, such requirements in our metal-model are considered from the initial SPL phases:

Uniform and first-class representation of variation points in all abstraction levels. Sinnema et al. (2004) stated that *"uniform and first-class representation of variation points facilitates the assessment of the impact of selections during product derivation and changes during evolution"*.

Hierarchical organization of variability representation. In (Sinnema et al., 2004), it is also argued that explicitly representing these variation points hierarchically reduces the cognitive complexity during the product derivation process.

Dependencies, including complex ones, should be treated as first-class citizens in the modeling approach. *"First class representation of dependencies can provide a good overview on all dependencies"*. In our metamodel, we provide mechanisms that enable all the SPL assets, even as all the dependencies, be treated as first-class citizens.

The interactions between dependencies should be represented explicitly. All the assets in a SPL should be linked in order to preserve their dependencies. By doing that, the product derivation, maintenance and evolution of the SPL can be performed in an efficient and effective way. Thus, the metamodel should have a very high degree of linkage among its entities.

In (Bühne et al., 2005), three (3) essential requirements were defined to support variability documentation across different SPLs. Although our metamodel is not intended to support multiple SPLs yet, one of those requirements may be useful:

Facilitate the creation of views on the documented variability and constraints. Bühne et al. (2005) stated that an approach to document and manage variability across SPLs needs *"to support selective retrieval of variability and commonality information, including variability constraints"*. It is not a specific cause when supporting different SPLs, but it is also important in a single SPL.

4.1 Traceability requirements

While analyzing all the previous requirements, we have noticed that *traceability* is the fundamental building block that enables those requirements. Thus, the basis for constructing a SPL metamodel is a strong linkage among all elements/assets involved in a SPL development. These elements, such as features, requirements, design, source code, and test artifacts, should be linked in a way that their building, evolution and maintenance could be more effectively controlled, and the impact of changes and addition of new features in different products from the SPL could be analyzed.

According to von Knethen & Paech (2002), tracing approaches should capture and manage relationships among the different documents built during development phase. It enables to support various stakeholders, such as maintainer, project manager, customers, developers, testers, etc., in performing their tasks. For example, project planners use traceability to perform impact analysis, while designers use it to understand dependencies between requirement and design (von Knethen & Paech, 2002). Thus, we believe that without enabling traceability as a basis of the metamodel, the realizations of the requirements previously described are not feasible, becoming the SPL development a complete disorder.

In (Bayer & Widen, 2001), some requirements are set that consider traceability issues: (a) *base the traceability on the SPL metamodel*; (b) *it should be customizable in terms of available trace types*; (c) *it should be capable of handling variability in the product line infrastructure*; (d) *the number of traces should be as small as possible*; and (e) *it should be automatable*.

Although we presented a large set of requirements along this section, we have not found studies that implement all these together. Thus, in our proposal, we grouped all these requirements to fit them in our metamodel, as detailed in next section. Furthermore, such requirements can also serve as a guideline for building SPL models.

5. The SPL metamodel

In this section, we describe the initial metamodel developed in order to fulfill the requirements specified in previous sections. It was developed using the UML notation (Booch et al., 2005). The metamodel was initially divided into *SPL management*, which currently includes the risk management sub-metamodel, and the *SPL core development*, which are the scoping, requirement, and tests sub-metamodels. Henceforth, we will call the submetamodels just by models.

Figure 4 shows the overall view of the metamodel, where the dashed boxes specify the models of the metamodel. The variability model is strongly based on the generic metamodel proposed by Bachmann et al. (2003). We split the metamodel into small diagrams in the next subsections in order to explain it in details. It starts by detailing the Asset UML Profile, scoping model, then moving towards requirement, tests, and management models.

5.1 Asset UML profile

This is the metamodel core entity, called *Asset*, as shown in Figure 5. This entity is used as a UML profile[3] for the other entities of the metamodel which should behave as an *Asset*. Thus, whenever an entity of the SPL metamodel have the properties of an *Asset*, it is extended using the *asset* profile tag. The usage of such profile has three main reasons: (1) to enable the evolution and maintenance of the metamodel without the need to modify the entire metamodel; (2) to transform the metamodel entities into first class entities; and (3) to keep the metamodel views clean and understandable.

The *Asset* entity is the metamodel core since it has properties that make feasible some of the requirements aforementioned. For example, it is related to a *History* entity, which is responsible to keep track of the changes that are performed in some *Asset* object. Thus, a *History* object records the *Asset* object which was modified, what kind of modification was performed, and who did it. Recording such modifications enables, for example, to calculate the probability that an *Asset* object has to be modified – such probability could impact directly in the SPL architecture design (von Knethen & Paech, 2002).

The *Asset* entity is also related to a set of metrics (*Metric* entity). During the SPL development, it is important to have information quantifying the metrics. For example, we could measure the effort for scoping analysis and requirement analysis, thus it would be possible to estimate the value for each feature or requirement. We could also set a metric for number of LOC (Lines of Code) for each feature in the SPL, or how many requirements and use cases some feature has. The granularity of the metrics can vary from the very high level to the very low level due to the strong tracking capability of the metamodel.

Furthermore, the *Asset* entity is also related to a *Version* entity. It enables the *Asset* objects to be versioned. This characteristic is important due to the variability nature of a SPL project. The presence of the *Version* entity means that for each modification in an *Asset* object, a new version

[3] UML profiles are an extension mechanism of the UML language (Booch et al., 2005) that allow models to be customized for specific domains.

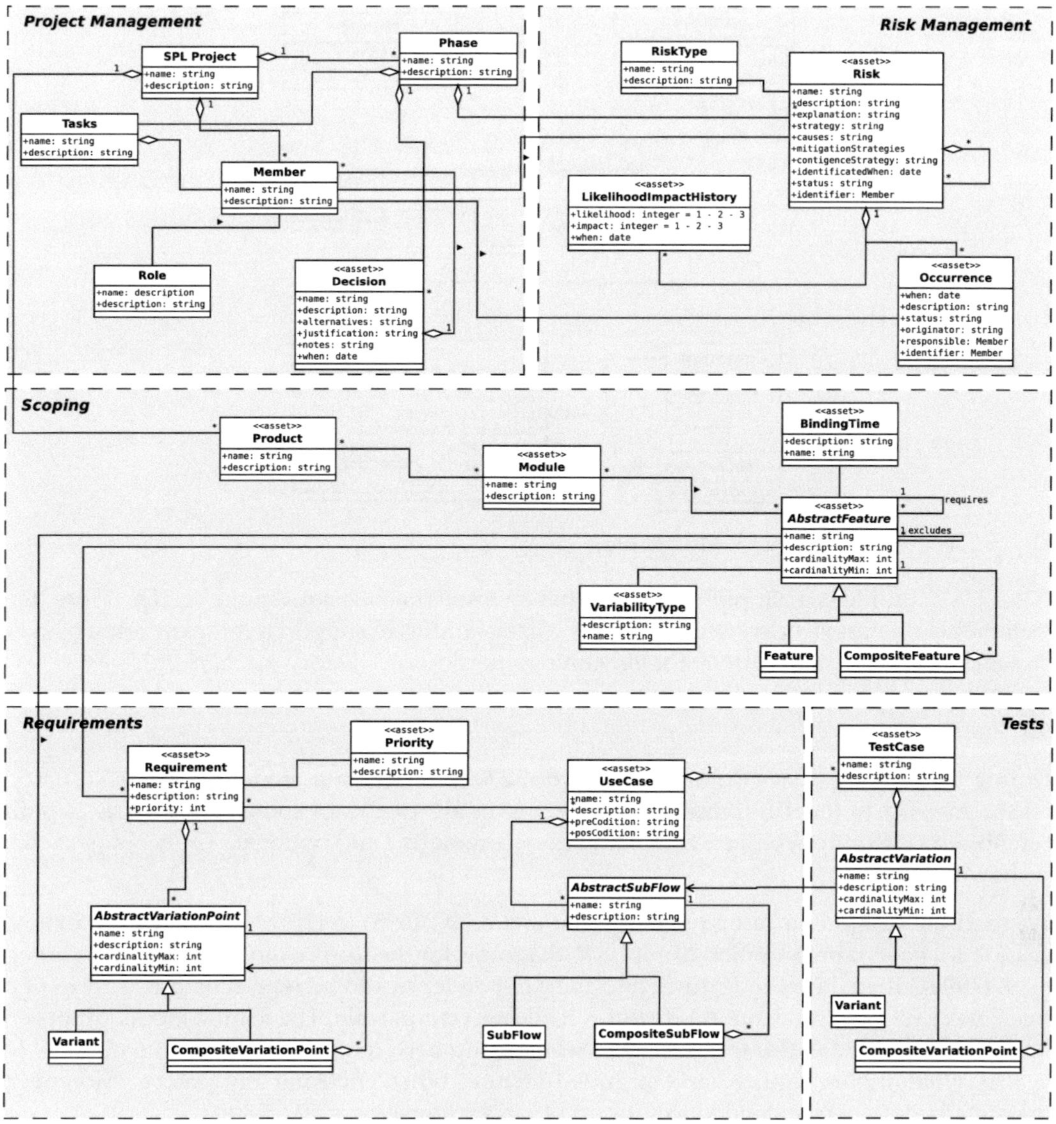

Fig. 4. Overview of the proposed SPL metamodel.

of this should be created. Thus, integrating a versioning mechanism inside the metamodel will enable easy maintenance of different versions of the same product. If the metamodel is extended to support different SPLs, it becomes more critical. The *History* entity should not be confused with the *Version* entity; the former holds metadata information for the *Asset* object, while the later keeps different copies of an *Asset* object.

Last, but not least, the metamodel also integrates a mechanism for issues reporting. This mechanism enables any *Asset* object to be associated with an *Issue* object. It also means that someone could report an issue for different versions of the same *Asset* object. As direct impact of this mechanism, it will provide easy maintenance and evolution of different *Asset* object versions. However, due to better understanding reasons, the issue mechanism showed in the

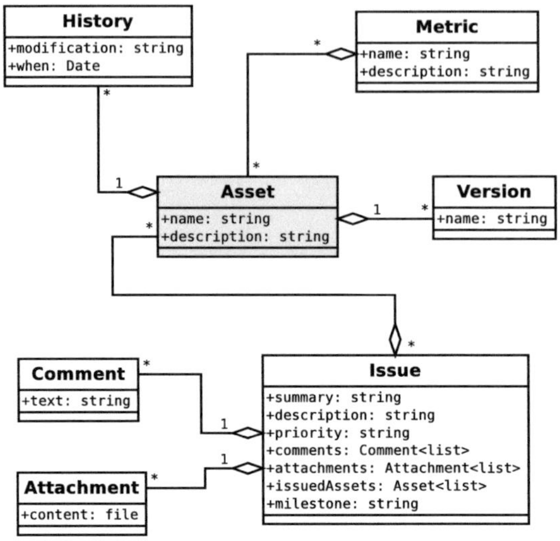

Fig. 5. The metamodel core UML profile.

Asset UML Profile is a simplification of what an issue mechanism should be. Therefore, the metamodel can be extended with other specialized entities to support a complete issue tracker system, even as it could be done for versioning, metrics, and history mechanisms.

5.2 Scoping model

During the scoping phase (John & Eisenbarth, 2009), the feature model is assembled based on the method to identify those features (Kang et al., 1990). In some cases, a tree is built containing all feature types, such as mandatory, alternative and optional. The scoping model is shown in Figure 6.

We used the Composite design pattern (Gamma et al., 1995) to represent the feature model, since it is a good representation using UML diagrams for the feature model proposed by Kang et al. (1990). It enables the features and their dependencies to be represented in a form of a tree, where features can have sub-features (children) recursively. The feature model proposed in the scoping model also enables other relationship between features, e.g. it is possible to specify what are the required and excluded features when choosing any feature. Moreover, the metamodel can be extended to support other relationships.

In the scoping model, a *Feature* object has *BindingTime*, *VariabilityType*, *Module* and *Product* entities associated with it. We did not specify the binding times and variability types for the features, because it must be done when instantiating the metamodel. According to Kang et al. (1990), examples of binding time are *before compilation*, *compile time*, *link time*, *load time*, *run-time*; and examples of variability type can be *Mandatory*, *Alternative*, *Optional*, and *Or*.

In the scoping model, the *Feature* objects are grouped into *Module* objects, and *Module* objects are then grouped into *Product* objects. The *Module* objects can be viewed also as the sub-domains of the *Product* objects. It was decided to structure the metamodel in this way since it better represents the SPL project we are developing in the mentioned private company. However, if it is not necessary to have a *Module* entity, it is easy to remove that from the metamodel, since the other phases are not directly linked to the *Module* entity.

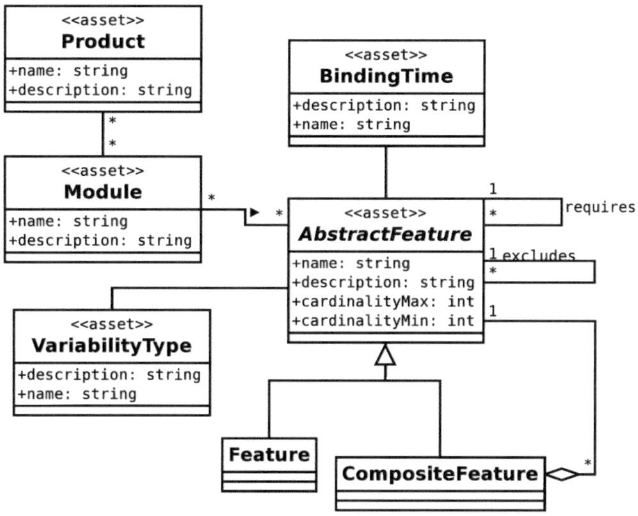

Fig. 6. The model for scoping phase.

5.3 Requirements model

The metamodel also involves the requirement engineering traceability and interactions issues, considering the variability and commonality in the SPL products. The two main work products from this SPL phase are the requirements and use cases. Figure 7 presents the model regarding the requirements phase.

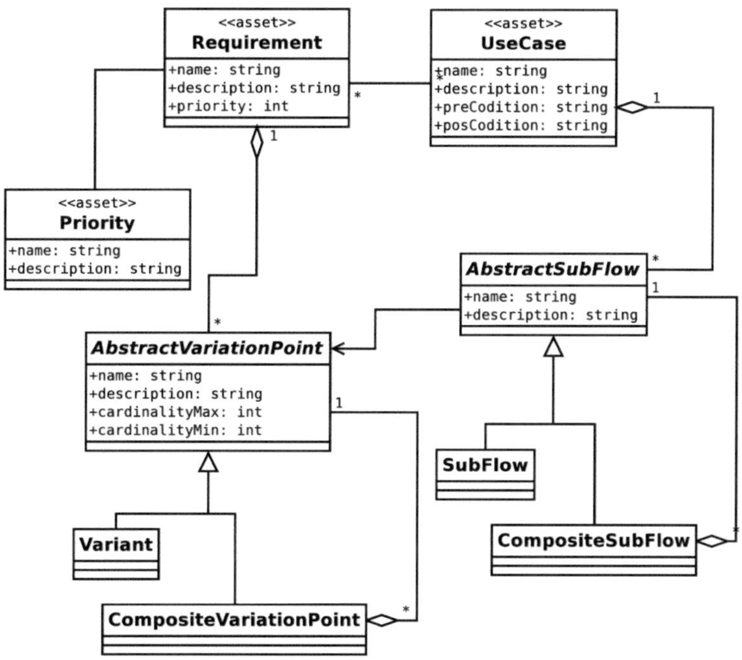

Fig. 7. The metamodel for requirements phase.

The *Requirement* object is composed by *name, description, bindingTime, priority*. During its elicitation, it should envisage the variations over the foreseeable SPL life-cycle (Clements & Northrop, 2001a), considering the products requirements and the SPL variations. Briefly, it presents what the systems should do and how they are supposed to be.

Some scoping outputs serve as source of information in this phase. For instance, during the requirements elicitation the feature model is one of the primary artifacts. Features and requirements have a many-to-many relationship, which means that one feature can encompass many requirements and different requirements can encompass many features (Neiva et al., 2009).

It is important to highlight that the metamodel was built in order to address the behavior of SPL projects. In this sense, there are three scenarios where a requirement may be described: *(i)* the requirement is a variation point; *(ii)* the requirement is a variant of a variation point; and *(iii)* the requirement has variation points.

The same scenarios are used when eliciting use cases, it also can be composed by variation points and variants, represented in the model by flow and sub-flow, respectively. In addition, the same many-to-many association is used between requirements and use cases, in which one requirement could encompass many use cases, and a use case could be encompassed by many requirements. The *UseCase* model is composed by *name, description, preCondition* and *postCondition*. The alternative flows are represented by the flows and sub-flows.

5.4 Tests model

The metamodel encompasses testing issues in terms of how system test cases interact with other artifacts. The *Test Cases* are derived from *Use Cases*, as can be seen in the metamodel and separated in Figure 8. This model expands on the abstract use case definition, in which variability is represented in the use cases. A use case is herein composed by the entity *AbstractFlow*, that comprises the subentity *Flow*, which actually represent the use case steps. Every step can be associated with a *subflow*, that can represent a variation point.

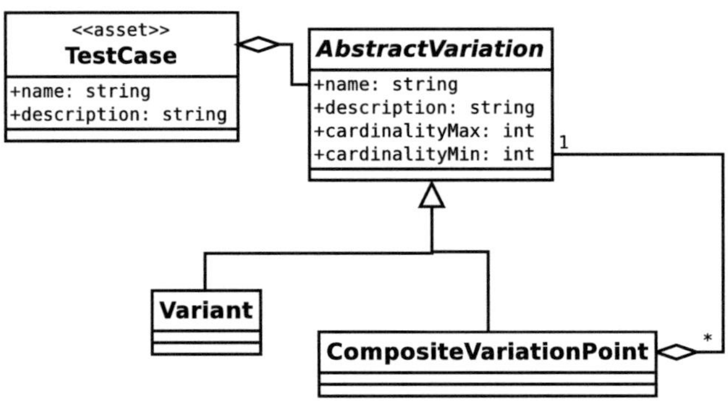

Fig. 8. The metamodel for tests.

Figure 9 illustrates the dependency between test objective and test case when variability is considered (Wübbeke, 2008). Consider that in (A) the component is variable as a whole, and in (B) only part of the component is variable. They will turn, respectively, into (A') and (B'), the former as a new test case, which is variable as a whole, and the latter, a test case in which only the corresponding part of the test case is variable.

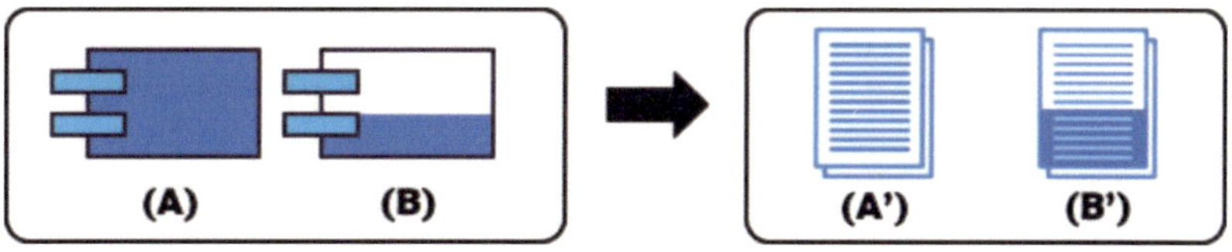

Fig. 9. Dependency between test objective and test cases considering variability.

Hence, the challenge is how to optimally build test cases that take into consideration variability aspects so that the reuse of the parts of test cases will emerge easily.

The case illustrated in the Figure 9 is a typical case, in which only part of a use case varies. It is not necessary to create different use cases to represent the variability, but rather reuse part of it. According to the requirements model of the metamodel (Figure 7), such a representation is feasible, since every step in a use case can make reference to a *subflow*.

Consider a hypothetical situation in which there are two variation points, the first representing an *optional feature* (white diamond), and the second representing an *alternative feature* (black diamond), as depicted by the diagram shown in Figure 10. This diagram represents five possible scenarios: (1) [A-B-C-D], (2) [A-B-C-D-E-F], (3) [A-B-C-D-E-G], (4) [A-E-F], (5) [A-E-G]. In this case, if we consider the first three possible scenarios, we could create the test case for scenario (1), and then reuse the flow of this scenario and the results for the remaining scenarios (2) and (3). This idea is brought from the control-flow coverage criteria, based on graph representation. We applied this same representation, but now considering aspects of variability.

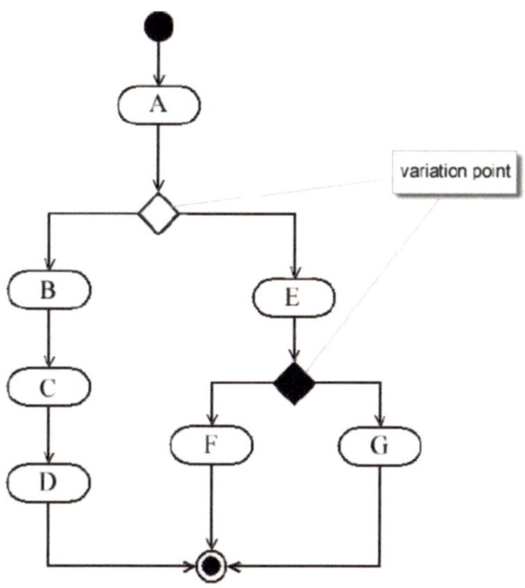

Fig. 10. Hypothetical diagram representing variability.

Considering that a use case can generate several test cases, the strategy to represent each step in a use case and enable it to be linked to a variation point enables the building of test cases which also consider the variation points. This way, several test cases can be instantiated from a use case, that have represented the variation points. Variability is preserved in the core asset test artifacts to facilitate reuse.

This strategy allows that every change in the use case and/or the variation points and variants to be propagated to the test cases and their steps (variable or not), due to the strong traceability represented in the metamodel.

5.5 Initial management model

In this section, the main characteristics of the management model are presented. The main objective of this model is to coordinate the SPL activities. Through this model it is possible to manage the SPL project and consequently keep track of its different phases and the staff responsible for that. Thus, it is possible to maintain the mappings and traceability between every artifact.

As illustrated in Figure 11, the management model can be viewed as the starting point to the SPL metamodel. Hence, through this model we can define information about the SPL project as well as details such as the SPL phases, the tasks to be performed, the members responsible for the tasks and their associated roles. In addition, the decisions about the SPL project can be documented using the Decision entity, by describing the alternatives, justification, notes, when it occurred, and the involved staff.

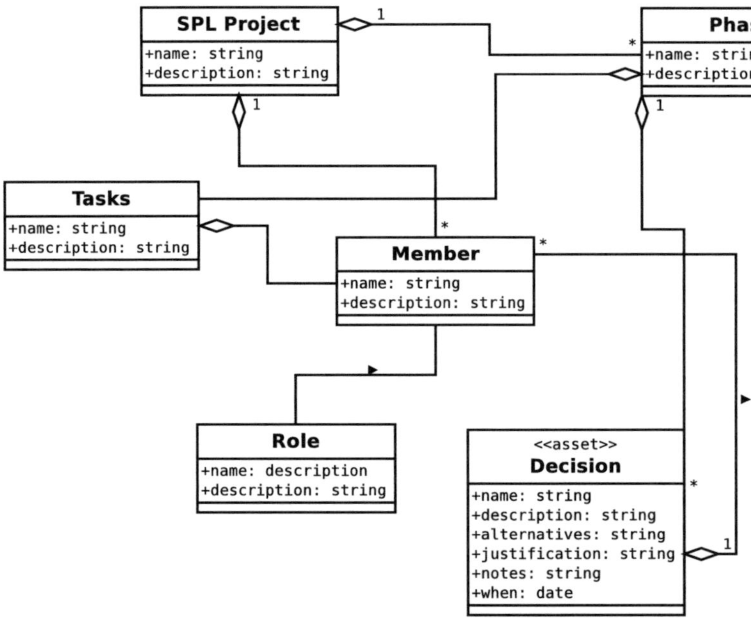

Fig. 11. The model for project management.

5.5.1 Risks model

According to Sommerville (2007), Risk Management (RM) is particularly important for software projects because of the inherent uncertainties that most projects face. These stem from loosely defined requirements, difficulties in estimating the effort and resources needed for software development, and dependence on individual skills and requirements changes due to changes in customer needs.

Thus, our RM model for SPL involves activities which must be performed during the RM process that involves all SPL phases. These activities are based on the definition proposed by Sommerville (2007), however it was adapted to our context, based upon the needs with feedback in risk identification stage. The following activities for RM should be performed:

1. *Risk identification:* it is possible to map the risks in the project, considering product and business risks identification;
2. *Risk Documentation:* identified risks are documented in order to provide the assessment of them;
3. *Risk analysis:* the likely to occur and the consequences of these risks are assessed;
4. *Risk planning:* plans to address the risk either by avoiding it or minimizing its effects on the project are drawn up;
5. *Risk monitoring:* the risk is constantly assessed and plans for mitigation are revised as more information about the risk becomes available.

These activities compose the base for the RM model proposed in our metamodel in a way that may support an automated risk management strategy. Figure 12 shows the functionalities encompassed by the RM model.

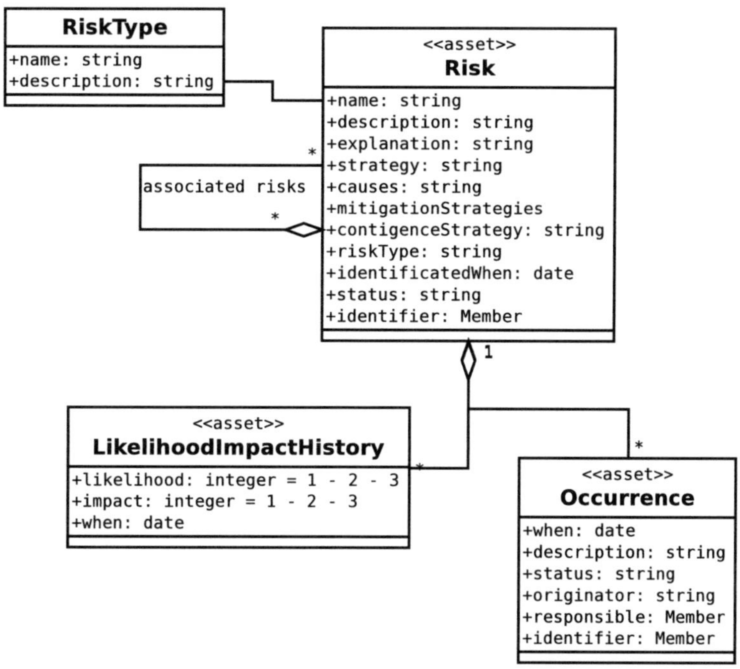

Fig. 12. The metamodel for risks management.

According to the RM model, the risks are identified and then their main characteristics are documented. The characteristics are: the risk description, type, status, mitigation strategy, and contingency plans. In addition, as the RM process is a continuous activity, it is necessary to keep track of the history about the management of these risks. Thus, the risks' likelihood and impact are documented according to their occurrence, which can happen in different moments throughout the project development. It is important to emphasize that our approach to risk management should be performed in the essential activities of the SPL: Core Assets Development (CAD), Product Development (PD) and Management (M).

6. Implementing and validating the metamodel

In order to validate the metamodel, we have implemented a web tool where all the entities from the metamodel are provided and specialized in the tool for the company settings, and the intended metamodel traceability is fully supported. We implemented the tool using the Django[4] framework, which enabled the fast development of a functional prototype. With Django implementation, we mapped the metamodel entities and their relationship within Python[5] classes, and then a relational database for these entities is automatically created. Finally, Django generates a Web application where it is possible to test the mapping by inserting some test data – in our case, the documentation regarding features, requirements and so on.

After this initial application generated by Django, we can extend it by developing new functionalities for the tool. Currently, it is possible to use the tool to document all the assets regarding the metamodel, however the test cases derivation from use cases is not supported yet. Furthermore, the tool is able to produce feature models visualizations, as well as product maps and other type of project documentation. For example, there are several types of reports that can be generated, such as: features per modules/products; all the features, requirements and use cases per modules/products; and the traceability matrix among these different assets.

Additionally, the tool also aids in the inspection activity – static quality assurance activities carried out by a group composed by the authors of the artifacts, a reader and the reviewers – through the generation of different reports and providing a way to gather information about the change requests that should be performed in the inspected artifacts. Moreover, it is important to mention that the tool provides a bug tracker, as proposed by the metamodel, in order to manage the change requests. This also enables the tool to store all the historical data to be further reused and serve as lessons learned in project future activities.

Since the tool provides the traceability proposed in the metamodel, it has also a way to measure the impact analysis of each change request. For example, given a change in a use case, the user opens a change request referencing that asset in order to solve that problem, then the Change Control Board will investigate the change and assign a responsible to fix it. As soon as someone starts to investigate the defect/enhancement, the tool can be asked to inform the impacted artifacts associated with that change in that specific use case. In this way, it can also help the decision regarding when a change should be done in the common platform or in a single SPL product.

The tool has been used inside the company mentioned in the initial sections, since July 2010. As previously stated, the project goal is to change their single software development process to a SPL process. The tool is currently being used by SPL consultants working embedded in the company to perform the scoping and requirements engineering phases. So far, it was documented 4 products, 9 modules, 97 features, 142 requirements and 156 use cases using the tool. In parallel, designing, implementation and testing are being started.

[4] `http://www.djangoproject.com`
[5] `http://www.python.org`

7. Others metamodels, approaches and tools

We searched the literature related work which addressed *metamodels for SPL* and/or *approaches and tools derived from the metamodels*. Hence, we briefly describe our findings in the following subsections.

7.1 Metamodels

In (Streitferdt, 2001), it is proposed a metamodel to integrate requirements to the feature model, such as the one proposed in (Kang et al., 1990). A requirement, in this case, is an indivisible piece of text describing some portion of the system to be developed. The requirements can be described hierarchically, thus achieving variability. Furthermore, the traceability among the entities is based on the metamodel itself.

In (Bachmann et al., 2003), a high level metamodel for representing variability in SPL is proposed. The major goal of the metamodel was to "*separate out the representation of variability from the representation of various assets developed in the product development lifecycle while maintaining the traceability between them*".

The authors in (Berg et al., 2005) proposed a conceptual variability model in order to address traceability of variations at different abstraction levels and across different generic artifacts of the SPL. To achieve that, it is proposed to represent the variability in a third dimension. In such dimension, the variations points would be linked to the generic artifacts (such as requirements, use cases, architecture, etc.) to keep the traceability.

In (Bühne et al., 2005), a metamodel is described to structure variability information across different SPLs. It also based the metamodel in a set of requirements to document requirements variability. Moon et al. (2007) introduced two metamodels representing domain requirements and domain architecture with variability, and the traceability between these artifacts are based upon the metamodel.

7.2 Approaches and tools

In (Dhungana et al., 2007), it is briefly described an integrated tool support to develop SPL. Such tool follows some requirements, such as: Domain-specific adaptations, Mining existing assets, Involving multiple teams, Project-specific adaptations, Support for product derivation, Capturing new requirements during derivation, and Supporting product line evolution. However, it is not discussed the metamodel behind it.

Alférez et al. (2008) proposed a model-driven approach for linking features and use cases, along with its activities, and an example about how to apply the approach was showed. The authors did not differentiate between requirements model and use case model, and it is not explicitly described how the flows and sub-flows of the use cases should be handle.

Jirapanthong & Zisman (2009) presented the XTraQue, which is a rule-based approach to support automatic generation of traceability relations. In the approach, the feature model, use cases and some design documents are represented using XML. Thus, the approach extracts the relationships from these documents automatically using predefined rules.

As it can be seen, the literature basically proposes metamodels or techniques that address only a specific portion of SPL development. In addition, traceability and variability are not always considered together, or the description and the details of them are very simplified. Thus, the main difference between the previous described work and our proposal, is that we present a metamodel, and the implementation of it, for SPL development concerning variability and traceability aspects together along the early phases of SPL, and providing a level of details that simplifies the adoption of the metamodel. Furthermore, the tool that implements our metamodel is currently being used in a industrial project.

8. Conclusion and future work

In this chapter, it was proposed a metamodel for Software Product Lines that encompasses several phases of a SPL development, representing the interactions among the assets of a SPL, developed in order to provide a way of managing traceability and variability, and its initial validation inside a private company. The metamodel was built based upon a real-world SPL project being conducted in a private software company from Brazil. The organization works in the healthcare management systems domain, and have essentially four products, counting a total of 102 modules (sub-domains), with encompass about 840 features.

The phases currently supported by the metamodel include: scoping, requirements engineering, and tests. Additionally, the metamodel also supports different management aspects of a SPL project. For example, in the current version of the metamodel it is possible to manage different SPL projects concerning the staff, phases and activities, and it is proposed a model for managing risks in SPL.

In the way that we conceived the metamodel, the assets are treated as first-class citizens, which means that we can trace the linkage of any asset to others. Furthermore, treating assets as first-class citizens in our metamodel also enables a set of issues: to keep different versions of the same asset concerning different products in the SPL; to keep the history of assets modifications; to associate any metrics to assets; and it is also possible to manage the defects for different versions of the assets. Furthermore, by incorporating the management model, it is also possible to keep track of different assets and their responsible.

Although the metamodel was conceived to represent the SPL project for a specific company, in which we have been working jointly, it was built to be adaptable to other contexts. For example, the metamodel can be easily changed to support single system development by removing SPL specific entities.

For future work, we intend to extend the metamodel to support more aspects of SPL development. Specifically, we are planning to extend the model for metrics management, detailed software configuration aspects, integrate a model for SPL architecture, and establish mechanisms to link all these artifacts to source code.

We also plan to provide some way to enable the products derivation. The reuse between different SPLs (Bühne et al., 2005) is also intended to be implemented in future releases of the metamodel. In addition, formalized evaluations will be performed, that consider aspects of empirical software engineering, in order to assess the metamodel effectiveness. Finally, the prototype initially created to support the metamodel should be evolved, as well as formally validated.

9. References

Alférez, M., Kulesza, U., Moreira, A., Araújo, J. & Amaral, V. (2008). Tracing from features to use cases: A model-driven approach, *VaMoS'08: Proc. of the 2nd International Workshop on Variability Modeling of Software-intensive Systems*, pp. 81–87.

Anquetil, N., Kulesza, U., Mitschke, R., Moreira, A., Royer, J.-C., Rummler, A. & Sousa, A. (2010). A model-driven traceability framework for software product lines, *Software and Systems Modeling* 9: 427–451.

Bachmann, F., Goedicke, M., do Prado Leite, J. C. S., Nord, R. L., Pohl, K., Ramesh, B. & Vilbig, A. (2003). A metamodel for representing variability in product family development, *PFE'03: Proc. of the 5th International Workshop on Software Product-Family Engineering*, pp. 66–80.

Bayer, J. & Widen, T. (2001). Introducing traceability to product lines, *PFE'01: Proc. of 3th International Workshop on Software Product-Family Engineering*, pp. 409–416.

Berg, K., Bishop, J. & Muthig, D. (2005). Tracing software product line variability: from problem to solution space, *SAICSIT'05: Proc. of the 2005 Annual Research Conference of the South African Institute of Computer Scientists and Information Technologists on IT Research in Developing Countries*, SAICSIT, Republic of South Africa, pp. 182–191.

Birk, A. & Heller, G. (2007). Challenges for requirements engineering and management in software product line development, *REFSQ'07: Proc. of the 11th International Working Conference on Requirements Engineering*, Springer-Verlag, Berlin, Heidelberg, pp. 300–305.

Booch, G., Rumbaugh, J. E. & Jacobson, I. (2005). *The Unified Modeling Language User Guide*, second edn, Addison Wesley.

Bühne, S., Lauenroth, K. & Pohl, K. (2005). Modelling requirements variability across product lines, *RE'05: Proc. of the 13th International Conference on Requirements Engineering*, pp. 41–52.

Cavalcanti, Y. C., do Carmo Machado, I., da Mota Silveira Neto, P. A., Lobato, L. L., de Almeida, E. S. & de Lemos Meira, S. R. (2011). Towards metamodel support for variability and traceability in software product lines, *Proceedings of the Fifth International WOrkshop on Variability Modeling of Software-Intensive Systems (VaMoS'2011)*, Namur, Belgium, pp. 49–57.
URL: *http://yguarata.com/blog/wp-content/uploads/2011/01/vamos2011_submission_30.pdf*

Clements, P. & Northrop, L. (2001a). *Software product lines: practices and patterns*, Addison-Wesley, Boston, MA, USA.

Clements, P. & Northrop, L. (2001b). *Software Product Lines: Practices and Patterns*, Addison-Wesley, Boston, MA, USA.

de Oliveira, Junior, E. A., Gimenes, I. M. S., Huzita, E. H. M. & Maldonado, J. C. (2005). A variability management process for software product lines, *Proceedings of the conference of the Centre for Advanced Studies on Collaborative research (CASCON)*, pp. 225–241.

Dhungana, D., GrALnbacher, P. & Rabiser, R. (2010). The dopler meta-tool for decision-oriented variability modeling: a multiple case study, *Automated Software Engineering* pp. 1–38.

Dhungana, D., Rabiser, R., Grünbacher, P. & Neumayer, T. (2007). Integrated tool support for software product line engineering, *ASE'07: Proc. of the IEEE/ACM International Conference on Automated Software Engineering*, pp. 533–534.

Gamma, E., Helm, R., Johnson, R. & Vlissides, J. (1995). *Design patterns: elements of reusable object-oriented software*, Addison-Wesley, Boston, MA, USA.

Jirapanthong, W. & Zisman, A. (2009). Xtraque: traceability for product line systems, *Software and System Modeling* 8(1): 117–144.

John, I. & Eisenbarth, M. (2009). A decade of scoping: a survey, *SPLC'09: Proc. of the 13th International Conference on Software Product Lines*, pp. 31–40.

Kang, K. C., Cohen, S. G., Hess, J. A., Novak, W. E. & Peterson, A. S. (1990). Feature-oriented domain analysis (foda) feasibility study, *Technical report*, Carnegie-Mellon University Software Engineering Institute.

Linden, F. J. v. d., Schmid, K. & Rommes, E. (2007). *Software Product Lines in Action: The Best Industrial Practice in Product Line Engineering*, Springer-Verlag New York, Inc., Secaucus, NJ, USA.

McGregor, J., Sodhani, P. & Madhavapeddi, S. (2004). Testing Variability in a Software Product Line, *SPLIT '04: Proceedings of the International Workshop on Software Product Line Testing*, Boston, Massachusetts, USA, p. 45.

Mohan, K. & Ramesh, B. (2007). Tracing variations in software product families, *Communications of the ACM* 50: 68–73.

Moon, M., Chae, H. S., Nam, T. & Yeom, K. (2007). A metamodeling approach to tracing variability between requirements and architecture in software product lines, *CIT'2007: Proc. of the 7th IEEE International Conference on Computer and Information Technology*, University of Aizu, Fukushima Japan, pp. 927–933.

Neiva, D. F. S., de Almeida, E. S. & de Lemos Meira, S. R. (2009). An experimental study on requirements engineering for software product lines, *EUROMIRCRO-SEAA'09: Proc. of the 35th Euromicro Conference on Software Engineering and Advanced Applications*, pp. 251–254.

Northrop, L. M. (2002). Sei's software product line tenets, *IEEE Software* 19(4): 32–40.

Pohl, K., Böckle, G. & Linden, F. J. v. d. (2005a). *Software Product Line Engineering: Foundations, Principles and Techniques*, Springer-Verlag New York, Inc., Secaucus, NJ, USA.

Pohl, K., Böckle, G. & Linden, F. J. v. d. (2005b). *Software Product Line Engineering: Foundations, Principles and Techniques*, Springer-Verlag, Secaucus, NJ, USA.

Ramesh, B. & Jarke, M. (2001). Toward reference models for requirements traceability, *IEEE Trans. Softw. Eng.* 27: 58–93.
URL: *http://dl.acm.org/citation.cfm?id=359555.359578*

Rilling, J., Charland, P. & Witte, R. (2007). Traceability in Software Engineering – Past, Present and Future, *Technical Report TR-74-211*, IBM Technical Report, CASCON 2007 Workshop.

Sinnema, M., Deelstra, S., Nijhuis, J. & Bosch, J. (2004). Covamof: A framework for modeling variability in software product families, *SPLC'04: Proc. of the 9th International Software Product Line Conference*, pp. 197–213.

Sommerville, I. (2007). *Software Engineering*, 8 edn, Addison Wesley.

Streitferdt, D. (2001). Traceability for system families, *ICSE'01: Proc. of the 23rd International Conference on Software Engineering*, pp. 803–804.

Svahnberg, M., van Gurp, J. & Bosch, J. (2005). A taxonomy of variability realization techniques: Research articles, *Software Practice and Experience* 35(8): 705–754.

von Knethen, A. & Paech, B. (2002). A survey on tracing approaches in practice and research, *Technical report*, Fraunhofer Institute of Experimental Software Engineering.

Wübbeke, A. (2008). Towards an efficient reuse of test cases for software product lines, *SPLC'08: Proc. of the International Conference on Software Product Lines*, pp. 361–368.

2

An Approach for Representing Domain Requirements and Domain Architecture in Software Product Line

Shahliza Abd Halim, Dayang N. A. Jawawi, Noraini Ibrahim and Safaai Deris
Software Engineering Department, Universiti Teknologi Malaysia, Skudai, Malaysia

1. Introduction

Software Product Line (SPL) core assets development is an effective approach in software reuse in which core assets can be shared among the members of the product line with an explicit treatment of variability. Among the artefacts of core asset are architecture, reusable software components, domain models, requirements statements, documentation and specifications, performance models, schedules, budgets, test plans, test cases, work plans, and process descriptions.Variability in its own right is the central concept in SPL which is not being catered by conventional method of reuse. Consequently, it is important for variability to be identified and to be represented early at requirements phase. The importance of identifying requirements variability earlier at requirements level is also known as systematic reuse by researchers (Frakes and Isoda 1994; Muthig 2002). Variability at requirements levels also initiates the existence of the variability at architecture thus further highlight the inadequacy of considering variability solely at architectural level. Therefore, considering on variability at architecture and its implementation level is not enough where the understanding of variability at the requirements level is also required (Yu, Akhihebbal et al. 1998; Moon 2005; Kircher, Schwanninger et al. 2006).

Nonetheless, there are challenges on relating variability at both abstraction levels where mapping of user requirements with the core assets for the adaptation process and derivation of core assets based on user requirements is a complex task (Matinlassi 2004; Dhungana 2006). This task is made difficult due to the dependencies among variants in architecture in order to fulfil a single customer's requirements (Bachmann and Bass 2001; Chastek 2001; Thiel and Hein 2002). Furthermore, the variability information assembled within the requirements phase should be able to support the following phase, the architecture design (Brown, Gawley et al. 2006). Consequently, the relationships between both abstraction levels are not always apparent especially between high level requirements artifacts and more specific and formal artifacts of architecture such as Architecture Description Language (ADL)(Medvidovic, Grünbacher et al. 2003). In addition, relating between requirements to architecture also requires design decision to be explicitly represented (Bosch 2004; Avgeriou, Kruchten et al. 2007). Avgeriou et al. further highlight the importance of design decision accompanying the architecture development. Without the first class representation of explicit knowledge and rationale as in design decision, it leads to knowledge vaporization phenomena as described by Bosh. It is further suggested by him software architecture should also consider composition of domain models, usage scenarios, feature and other elements, which support architectural design decision.

In order to address the issues in relating between different abstraction levels, researchers proposed different views represented by different models with defined mappings between the models. The usage of multiple modeling and mappings are done by (Savolainen, Vehkomäki et al. 2002; Medvidovic, Grünbacher et al. 2003; Lee and Kang 2004; Savolainen, Oliver et al. 2005; Dhungana 2006; Sochos, Riebisch et al. 2006; Zhang, Mei et al. 2006; Zhu, Yuqin et al. 2007; Gomaa and Shin 2008; Bragança and Machado 2009; Lin, Ye et al. 2010). Among the approaches, Gomaa and Shin has the most comprehensive models used in their mappings (Gomaa and Shin 2008). Nevertheless, they only considers mapping at requirements to analysis model and do not involve mapping at architectural levels. There are also approaches which only concentrate on the rule and also the formal representation of the mapping without using any explicit models to represent the different abstraction levels (Savolainen, Oliver et al. 2005; Zhu, Yuqin et al. 2007). Furthermore, the mapping to architecture is generally referred as architectural assets and no specific elements mentioned at the architectural level. Another approach is by feature-driven mapping which is among the most accepted approaches so far by researchers (Lee and Kang 2004; Dhungana 2006; Sochos, Riebisch et al. 2006; Zhang, Mei et al. 2006; Lin, Ye et al. 2010). Nevertheless, these approaches seldom have an explicit representation of design decisions in order to records decisions that architects made while designing the domain architecture.

Therefore, even though the above-mentioned approaches for transitioning requirements models to architecture levels have proposed techniques to overcome majority of the issues mentioned earlier, nevertheless there are still room for improvement in the focus on of both functional and non-functional requirements which are essential elements for architecture development and also on the transition process itself which cannot be fully automated thus highlighting the importance of design decision in bridging between requirements and architectural level (Paech, Dutoit et al. 2002; Kaindl and Falb 2008; Turban, Kucera et al. 2009). However, we only elaborate on design decision at the conceptual framework only and both requirements and architecture level representation will be the center of attention instead in this chapter.

The layout of this chapter is as follows: Section 2 discusses the conceptual framework and process governing the representation of domain requirements and domain architecture. In Section 3, metamodels representing domain requirements level will be discussed. Discussion on the metamodels representing domain architecture level is described in Section 4. Section 5 illustrates the usage of the representation in Autonomous Mobile Robot Product Line case study. Section 6 discusses on the evaluation of the proposed notation. Lastly, Section 7 concludes this chapter.

2. Conceptual framework for bridging between domain requirements and domain architecture

In order to address the issues of integrating functional, non-functional, architecture and design decisions in relating between the two abstractions levels, we argue that SPL architecture design method should incorporate multiple model approach in order to relate the requirements elements to architectural elements. Multiple model approach can provide different views of the system for different stakeholders. Furthermore, in order to have a clear identification and representation for requirements to enable it to be of importance at the latter development phase, we investigate the knowledge suitable to be incorporated in domain requirements profile and also at domain requirements profile for the purpose of assisting the domain architecture representation development. Therefore, the research question to be answered in this book chapter is *"What are the representations suitable for representing core assets at domain requirements level?"* and *"What are the representations suitable for representing core assets at domain architectural level?"*

The conceptual framework for relating from requirements to architecture follows the framework proposed by Garlan, Capilla and Babar (Garlan 2000; Capilla and Ali Babar 2008) as shown in Figure 1. Garlan proposed an architecture representation by incorporating ADL in object oriented modeling UML.Whereas, Capilla and Babar proposed on three different elements should be incorporated in a decision mode the product constraints, variability and binding.

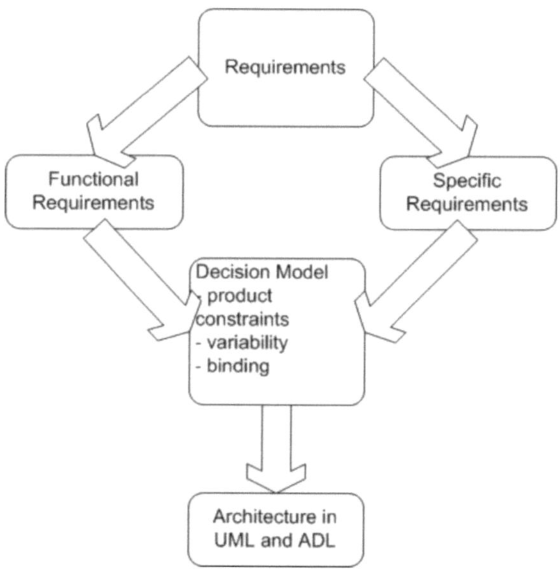

Fig. 1. Conceptual Framework for relating between requirements model to architecture

In order to represent the requirements and architectural elements representation, we use the extension provided in SysML profile (SysML 2006). SysML has extended UML 2.0 with specialized support for requirements engineering and traceability elements between requirements model and other models elements thus making it a perfect candidate in support of the variability extension. Furthermore, traceability support in SysML can contribute to the possibility of mapping between requirements and architectural level being done in the language. Section 3 and Section 4 will elaborate more on the treatment and mapping for each model.

Based on Figure 2, except for **Requirements Context** which is a matrix table to analyse requirements commonality and variability, **Use Case model, Parametric model** and **Feature Model** are multiple models for representing Domain Requirements. Parametric diagram is a new diagram extension in SysML to represent constrain on the property or behavior of a system (Friedenthal, Moore et al. 2008; Holt and Perry 2008). The diagram is used for representing system equations that can constrain the properties of a block (Friedenthal, Moore et al. 2008). Though the model is usually used to represent constraint in terms of mathematical equations it has the potential to be extended to represent general rule or to apply for requirements validation and verification. Figure 2 shows the association between the domain requirements model and the domain architectural model where design decision is the connection which link between the models. Decision model is where the functional and non functional constraint is being specified. There are also two types of mapping based on the figure, horizontal mapping refers to mapping between models at the same level of abstraction, in this case at domain requirements level (between use case, feature and parametric model). Vertical mapping refers to the mapping between different levels of abstractions, between domain requirements model and domain architecture model. Decision model will be the intermediate model between both abstraction levels.

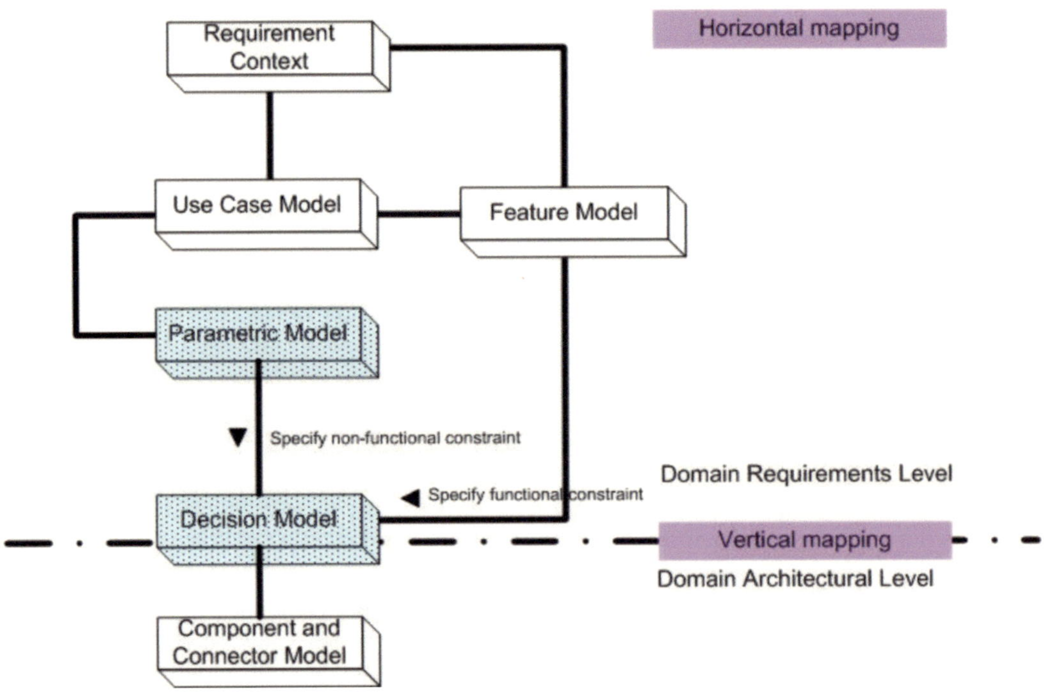

Fig. 2. Model for associating domain requirements to domain architecture with decision model

The lack of fundamental process models and guidelines for the transition between the two abstraction levels, further hinders the systematic task in developing the architecture. In order to have a clear process for relating between requirements to architecture in SPL, we look into available PLA design methods itself on their support for an explicit functional and non functional requirements and its transition for architecture design. Existing method for Product Line architecture design based on comparison by Matinlassi (Matinlassi 2004) has evaluated COPA, FAST, FORM, KobrA and Quality Driven Architecture Design and Analysis (QADA). From the evaluation, QADA method has consideration on quality attributes requirements. We have also reviewed books on SPL such as by (Gomaa 2005) concentrating on Product Line UML based Software Engineering (PLUS) method and by Bosch proposing Functionality based Architecture Design (FAD) method (Bosch 2000).

From the reviews there are only two architecture design methods that focus on functional and non-functional requirements, QADA and FAD. However, we concentrate on FAD as a process in our research as it provides clear description of its Product line Architecture process. Though FAD has a concentration in functional and non-functional requirements, yet it still does not show explicitly what are the techniques or methods involve for the process at the requirements level. Based on Figure 3, we will add suitable methods for each part of the processes in FAD (i.e. requirements specification, software architecture, design decision, derivation and mapping and lastly the evaluation or assessment done to the architecture).

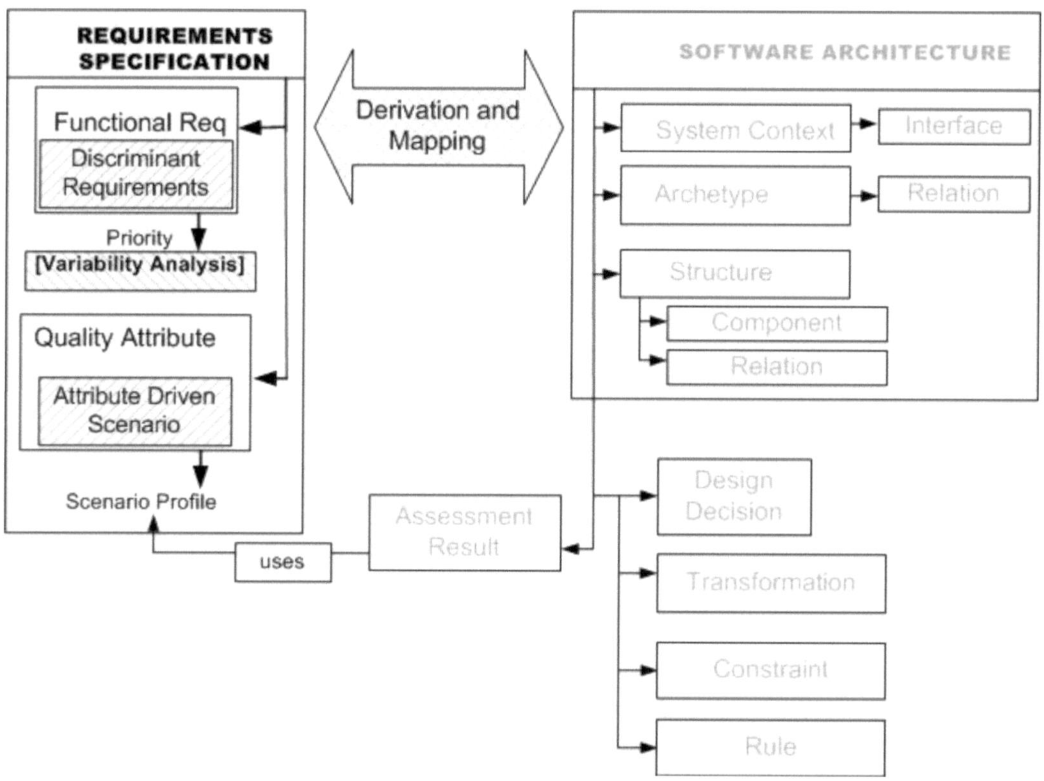

Fig. 3. Process for associating domain requirements to domain architecture adapted with enhancement from (Bosch 2000)

3. Metamodel for representing core assets at requirements level

Due to the unstructured nature of requirements, there are several approaches which combined different strategies in order to represent artifacts in requirements analysis for SPL. A systematic review has reported the high usage of textual and features artifacts in domain analysis followed by use cases and goal based methods and others (Mahvish and Tony 2009). Albeit the popular usage of feature model by various researches in SPL, it does not properly represent variability information (Bühne, Lauenroth et al. 2004; Moon 2005). Among the variability information that could not be supported by feature model are such as proper decision on choosing features as either common or optional, identification of variation points and also variation point type (Moon 2005) and required behavioral information in its representation (Brown, Gawley et al. 2006). Goal based strategy also has been reportedly having its own problem of implementation such as the abstractness of its concept has leads to the problem in finding the right goal (Aurum and Wohlin 2005). Thus, in our research, we concentrate on determining objectively the common and variable feature based on the analysis on existing similar applications. To achieve the objectivity, commonality and variability matrix is used in order to identify which are the common and optional requirements (Mikyeong, Keunhyuk et al. 2005; Halim, Jawawi et al. 2009). In order to complement the use of feature model, use case model is chosen as it enables the representation of text based system behavior (Armour, Miller et al. 2001).

a. Functional mapping

For functional mapping, the feature model is used for representing functional requirements while use case represents the behavioral specification of the requirements. Use case model have two extensions to its metamodel where use case documentations have been added with extra parameters for describing quality attributes. The extensions are shaded in grey as shown in Figure 4. Another extension is on use case types to identify priority and reuse property of the use case. For example if the priority is high the use case is a common and will be reused by all the application in the product line.

FODA is commonly used as feature model by researcher, however in this research, feature metamodel MRAM/TRAM is used as it has already proposed an extension of SysML profile (Mannion and Kaindl 2008). The metamodel contains discriminants which are features that differentiate one system from another. Discriminant and its associated pattern comprise of single adaptor, multiple adaptor and option. The stereotypes <<MA>> represent multiple adaptors, where at least one of the requirements can be chosen, while <<SA>> represent Single Adaptor variability where only one requirement can be chosen from the variants. Furthermore, MRAM/TRAM paired parameters and discriminant for modeling qualitative and quantitative variability. According to (Magnus, Jurgen et al. 2009), discriminant provide a decision model for composing product specification from product line requirements documentation. Figure 4 shows the mapping between use case model and feature model.

b. Non functional mapping

For representing non functional requirements, architecture scenario is used (Clements, Bachmann et al. 2003; Liming, Babar et al. 2004; Oquendo, Warboys et al. 2004; Bachmann, Bass et al. 2005). With the use of architecture scenario, the non functional requirements can be represented with more attribute instead of using just a general description or only using one word such as Performance, Modifiability or Security. The architecture scenario comprise of six elements which we will further refer as non functional parameters: stimulus; source of stimulus; environment; artifact, response; response measure and expected response .(Bass, Clements et al. 2003). Previously, architecture scenario has been proposed as design decisions and non functional requirements by (Zhu and Gorton 2007). However, our practice of using architecture scenario is in parametric diagram where it explicitly shows the non functional parameters of the architectural scenario. To enable non functional parameters to be defined in parametric diagram, it has to be defined prior to its usage. The metamodel of the parametric diagram is based on Holt and Perry (Holt and Perry 2008).

c. Horizontal mapping

The functional mapping between use case and feature metamodel is referred as in Figure 4 and also (non-functional mapping) between use case and parametric metamodel in Figure 5 as horizontal mapping. Hence, horizontal mapping is between models at the same level of abstraction, in this case at domain requirements level. In use case metamodel, we refer Extension Point metaclass as a variation point in use case model and also Discriminant metaclass as a variation point in Feature model. Thus, based on Figure 4, we have defined the mapping between variation points at use case model with variation point at feature model.

For the mapping between use case and parametric metamodel in Figure 5, the mapping is more superficial due to the nature of non – functional requirements which not usually exist in each use case. Furthermore, non-functional requirements also known to have an impact to one whole application and again there is no specific use case that can show this type of information. Thus, we will dwell further into this matter as our future research.

4. Metamodel for representing core assets at architectural level

UML has been used as an architecture modeling language and also a de facto modeling language used in the industry, even so there are arguments concerning its modeling notations inadequacy for representing architecture (Medvidovic, Rosenblum et al. 2002; Medvidovic, Dashofy et al. 2007). Another paradigm, which has a consistent, complete and correct architecture description for representing architecture is by using Architecture Description Language (ADL) (Taylor, Medvidovic et al. 2009).

Integrating both languages, ADL and UML can be considered as having a synergistic relationship where the combination enables a precise and explicit architecture description and at the same time having a wider usage among UML users in commercial tool. xADL is chosen due to its specialized schema targeted for product line architecture description (Dashofy, Hoek et al. 2005) while SysML is chosen due to its first class consideration for requirements modeling and also its traceability elements between requirements model and other models elements.

a. Mapping of SysML to xADL

The metamodel of the xADL and SysML integration have been proposed in (Halim, Jawawi et al. 2009). We have divided the profile into three sections, the metaclass section which consists of UML classes reused in SysML known as UML4SysML. The architectural construct section which shows the extension of stereotype classes and the variability construct section which shows the extension of stereotype to represent variability.

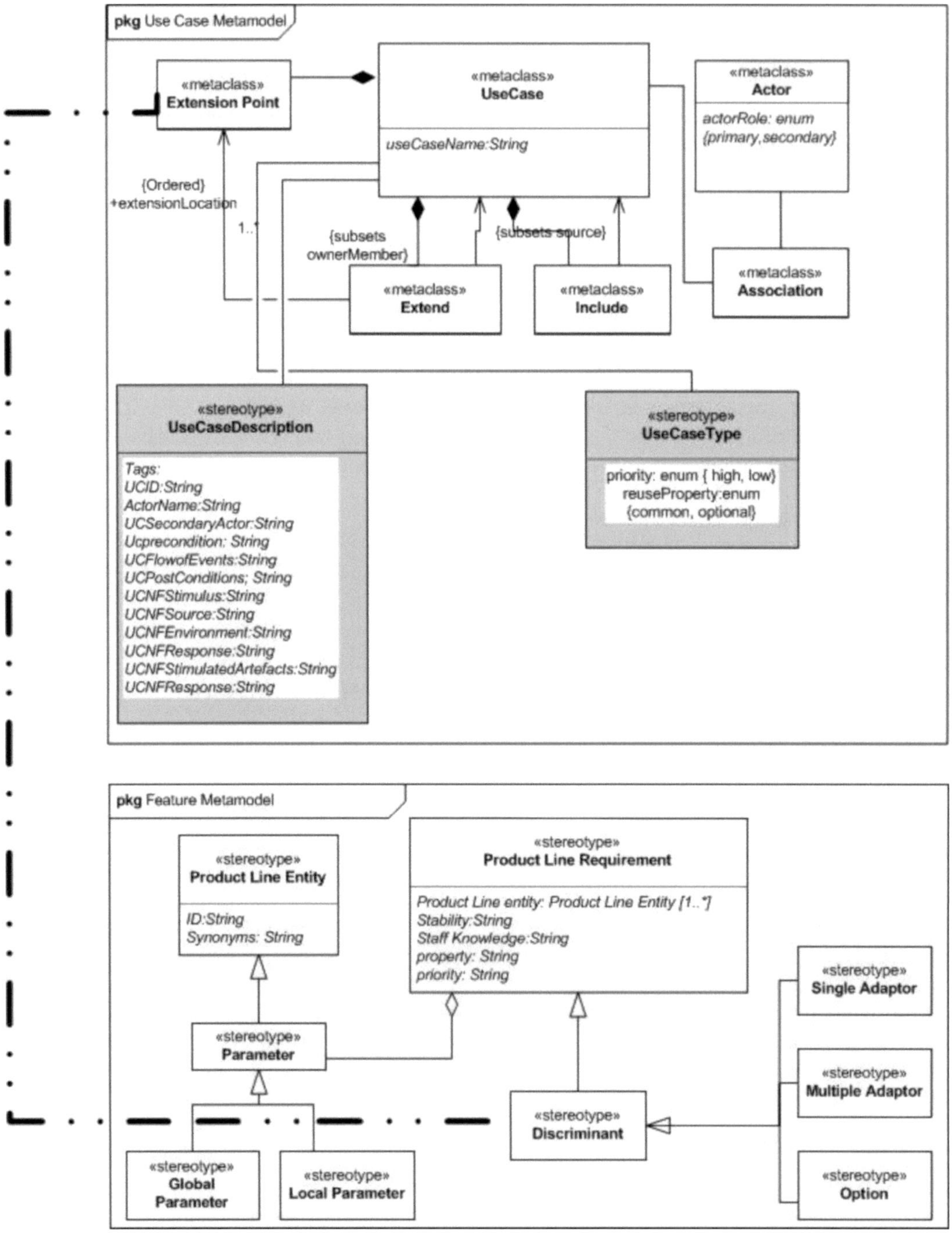

Fig. 4. Horizontal Mapping between use case and feature model

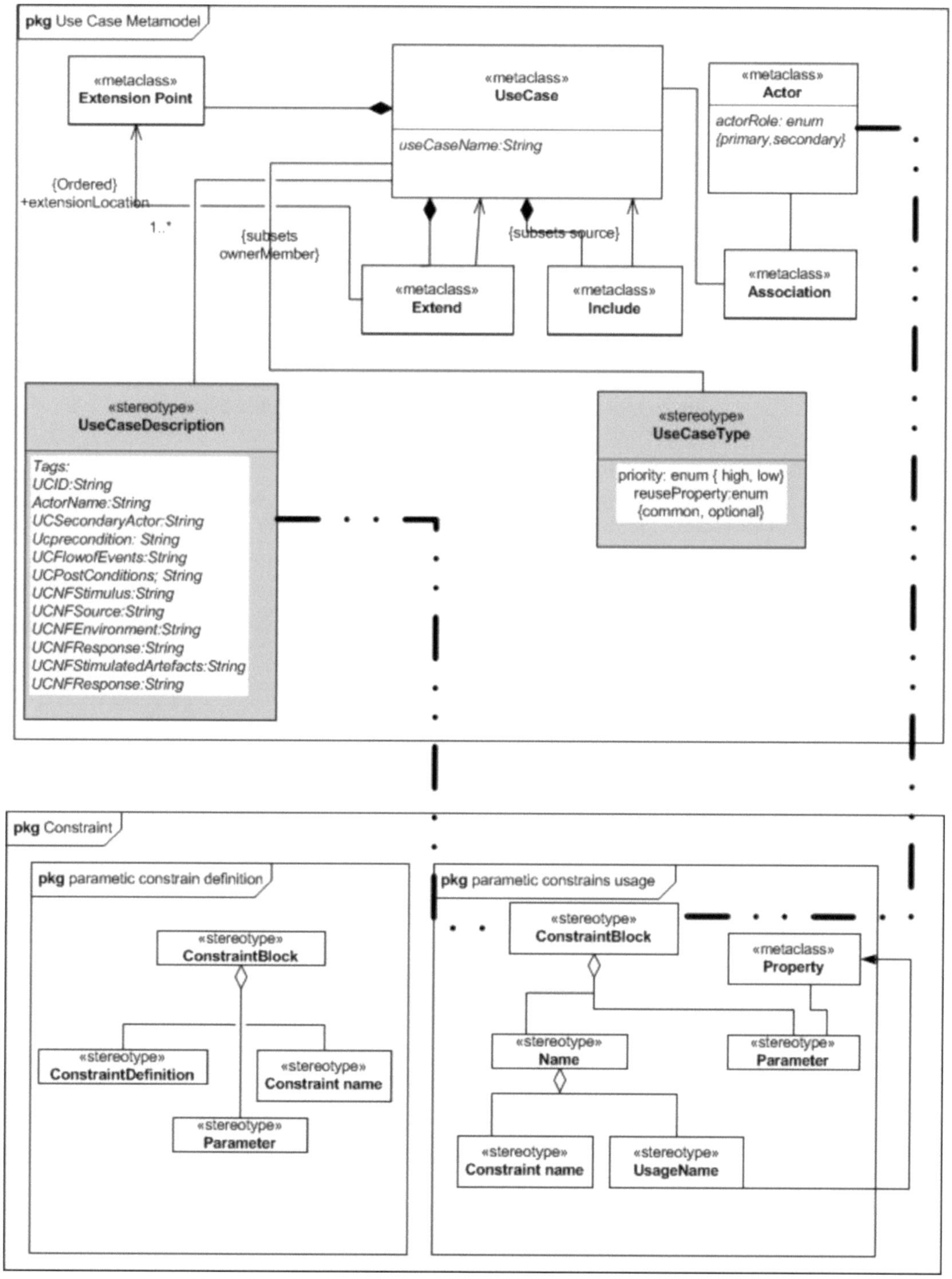

Fig. 5. Horizontal Mapping between use case and parametric model

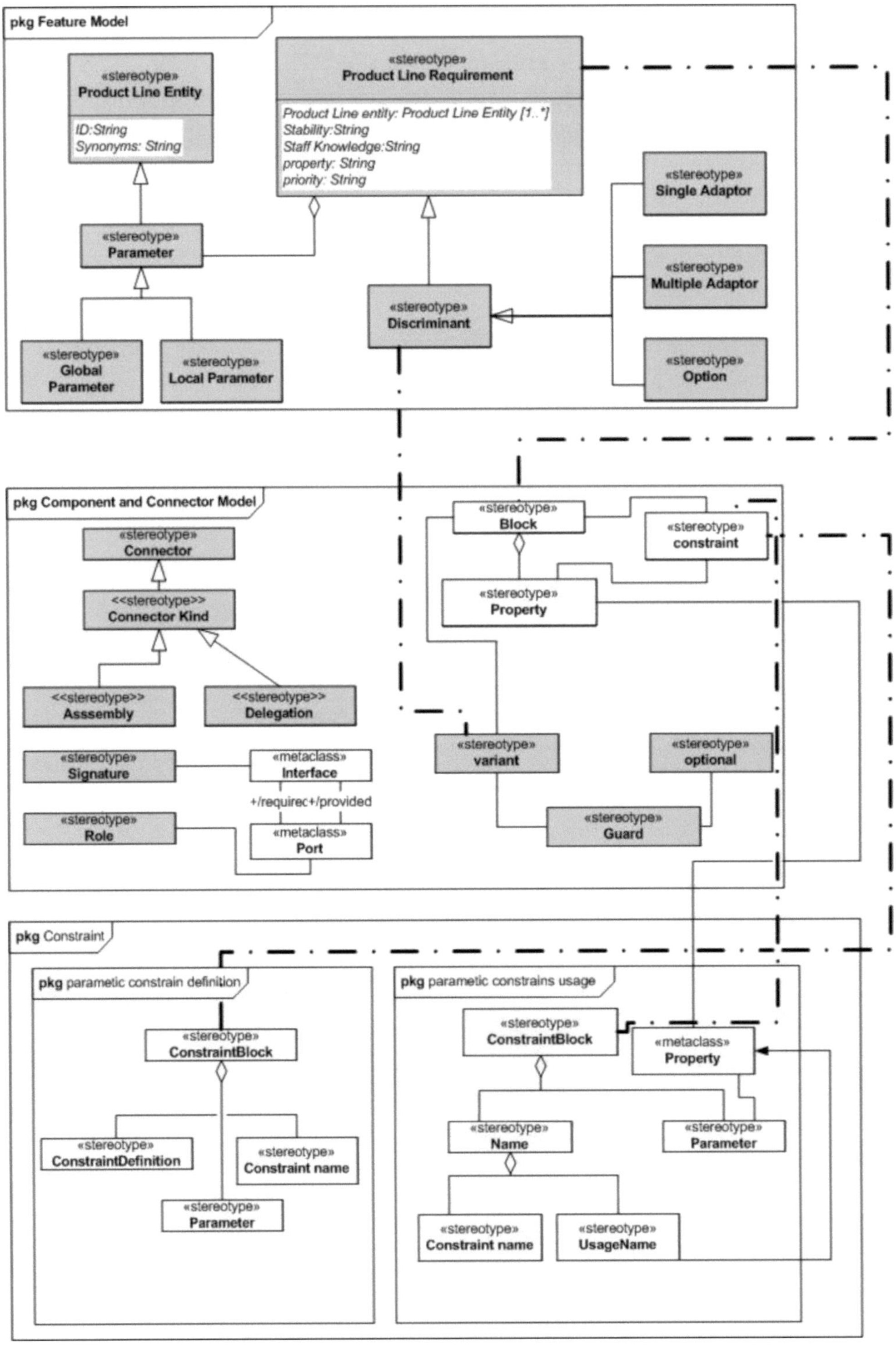

Fig. 6. Vertical Mapping between Domain Requirements to Domain Architecture

b. Vertical Mapping

Referring back to Figure 2, there should be a vertical mapping between domain requirements model (feature and parametric model) with the domain architecture model. However, the mapping involved decision model as an intermediate layers between the two abstraction levels. Due to the insufficient research result for decision model, the vertical mapping is done without considering decision model. Though the decision model does not exist, the vertical mapping shown in Figure 6 can be a future reference for capturing traceability information for the decision model.

The vertical mapping between the Feature metamodel to the component and connector metamodel is basically between the Discriminant metaclass to the Variant metaclass in Component and Connector metamodel. The mapping between the parametric diagram and the component and connector architecture is based on the constraint in the Block metaclass which can be matched to the *ConstraintBlock* metaclass in the Parametric metamodel.

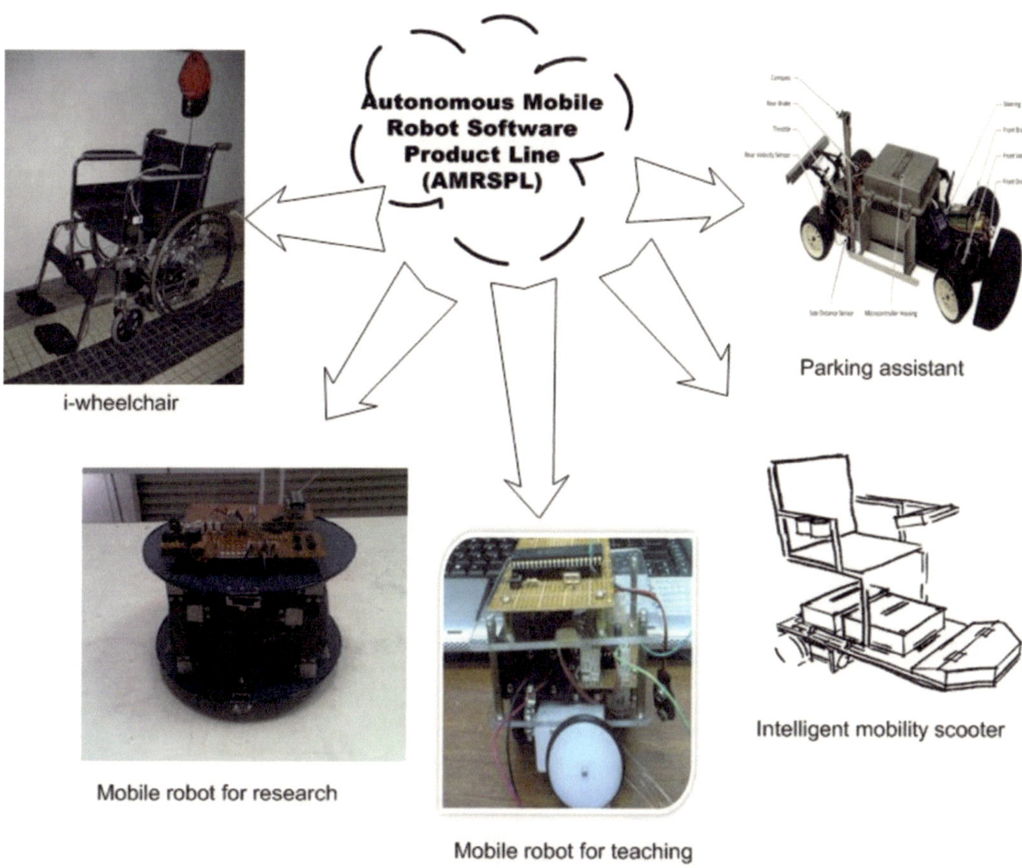

Fig. 7. AMR Product Line (AMRPL)

5. Case study of autonomous mobile robot software product line

In order to validate the applicability of the extended modelling in SysML, the extended model was applied to product line of Autonomous Mobile Robots (AMR). The product line consists of five different but similar applications of AMR. Four of the AMR are AMR for research, AMR for teaching, i-wheelchair and intelligent scooter based on the research collaboration done at Embedded Real Time and Software Engineering Research Lab (ERetSEL), Universiti Teknologi Malaysia. The fifth AMR is the parking assistant based on the work of Polzer, Kowalewski and Botterweck (Polzer, Kowalewski et al. 2009). The AMRPL is as shown in Figure 7.

In order to identify the commonality and variability of the AMRPL requirements, approach by Abd Halim, Jawawi and Safaai (Halim, Jawawi et al. 2009) is used. However, in order to simplify this paper, the common and variable function is represented in use case diagram as shown in Figure 8.

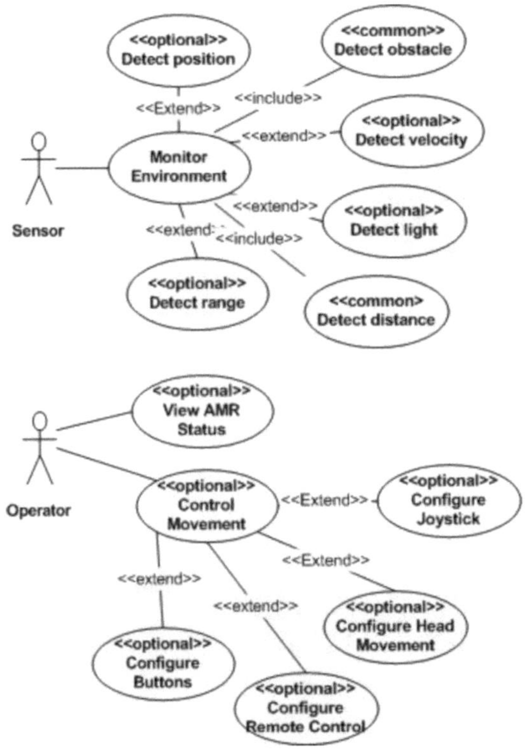

Fig. 8. AMRPL Use Case

Figure 9 shows all the three models based on their corresponding metamodel in Figure 6. Feature model represents the functional requirements in the form of SysML requirements model. Feature model in Figure 9 shows only partial requirements for AMRPL. The stereotypes <<MA>> represent multiple adaptors, where at least one of the requirements can be chosen, while <<SA>> represent Single Adaptor variability where only one requirement can be chosen from the variants. The ellipse shape for variants in Motor

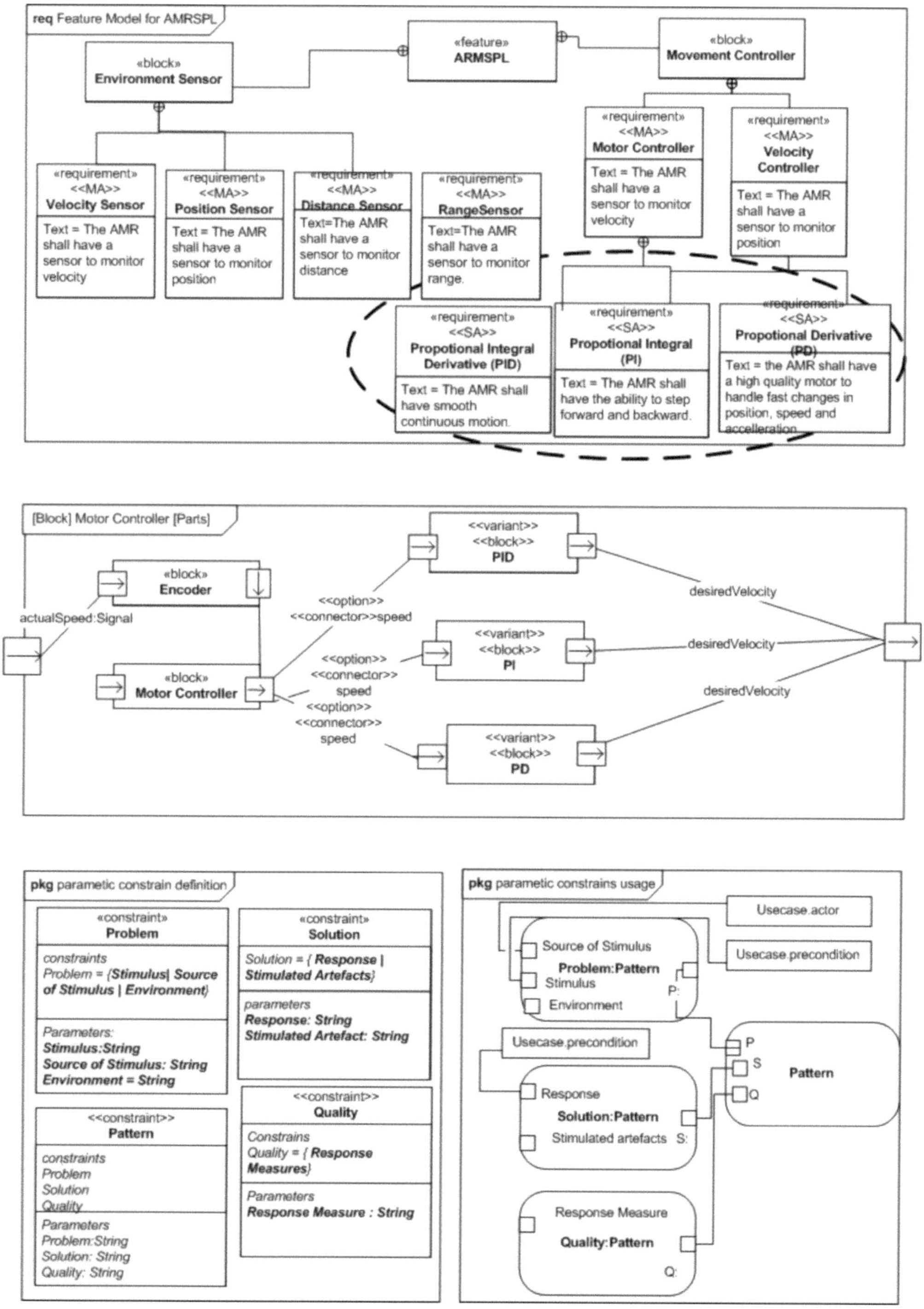

Fig. 9. Vertical mapping betweeen Feature Model, Parametric Model and Component Connector Model of AMRPL

Controller such as PID, PI and PD has been elaborated in the same name as in component and connector model. Non functional requirements are shown in parametric model in Figure 9. The parametric model is divided into definition and usage constraint. Parametric model in Figure 9 basically have defined four constraints. The parametric model represents the architecture scenario and how the scenario helps in identifying suitable patterns (Liming, Babar et al. 2004; Oquendo, Warboys et al. 2004). The pattern identified can then be used for later refinement of the initial architecture in the component and connector model.

6. Discussion

Based on the applicability of the proposed approach in modeling the domain requirements and domain architecture for AMRPL, we evaluate our proposed models and annotation in previous sections with suitable evaluation criteria. As far as our concern, there are two existing evaluation frameworks for evaluating variability modeling (Djebbi and Salinesi 2006; Sinnema and Deelstra 2007). The former proposed eleven criteria for comparing requirements variability modeling notations resulted from a brainstorming session with stakeholders. The evaluation framework is then compared to four feature-based notations FOPLE, FeatuRSEB, GP and FORE. The latter, concentrates on classifying variability modeling techniques based on two key characteristics. The key characteristics are representation for the variability itself and the tool accompanying the variability modeling (Sinnema and Deelstra 2007). Due to our variability modeling approach is based on profile extension, therefore the evaluation suitable for our approach is based on the extensions and the notations proposed in modeling the variability. Thus, we based our evaluation on the first evaluation framework proposed by Djebbi and Salinesi. The second evaluation framework by Sinnema and Deelstra is unsuitable for evaluating our approach as it rely heavily on the use of tool for the evaluation.

From the eleven criteria in the evaluation framework, we have classified the criteria into three classifications concerning our proposed notation. The three classifications are evaluation criteria fit for the notation, evaluation criteria for future extension of the notation and evaluation criteria which not covered by the notation. Evaluation criteria that fall into the first classification are readability of the notation, simplicity and expressiveness of the notation, explicit variability types of the notation, specification for variation point property, unified modeling of the notation and standardize notation. Second classifications, the future extension for the notation consist of criteria such as dependencies representation between the variable part of the product line, scalability of the notation and also the tool which support the proposed notation. The third classification is for the criteria which are not considered in our approach. Among the criteria are the evolution support of the product line and the adaptability of the notation towards other companies. Hence, we evaluate our notation based on the first classification only and the second and third classification will not be elaborated as it is either not being implemented yet or not related to our proposed notation.

Notations readability can be achieved by clear and minimal representation. The case study showed in previous section confirms visualization of variability at requirements and architectural level by using stereotypes. These elements thus demonstrate the clear representation of the notation. However, this notation has redundancy on information representing functional and non-functional requirements such as the information from use case to parametric diagram. This redundancy affect the minimality of the notation. For simplicity and expressiveness criteria, the construct proposed in the metamodel can be considered as sufficient to represent variability at requirements and architectural level. Though there are multiple models involve in representing domain requirements and domain architecture, however the number of entities in the metamodel are higher than the number of its relations thus highlight the simplicity of the notation. Expressiveness criteria have possibility to be achieved as the notation is based on extension from UML constructs therefore it can be understood by the user without much explanation. However, new model such as parametric diagram will have a significant effort for comprehension.

Evaluation criteria fit for the notation	
Readability of the notation	Metamodel mapping and UML based notations help in defining the graphical means to visualize domain requirements and domain architecture. However, there is possible duplication on information representing functional and non-functional requirements.
Simplicity and expressiveness of the notation	Simplicity can be achieved with the minimal construct in the metamodel to show variability. SysML profile which is an extension of UML reflects the expressiveness criteria.
Explicit variability types of the notation	Variability types at requirements and architectural levels are considered.
Specification for variation point properties	The proposed notation has a clear representation for variability through the use of stereotypes in the notation.
Case tool support	SysML profile extension is conformed to standard UML hence can also be supported by existing UML tool.
Unified modeling of the notation	Notations at requirements level have traceable relationships to notations at architectural level.

Table 1. Evaluation criteria fit for the notation

The notation can fulfill the third evaluation criterion, by having an explicit variability type at requirements level such as in use case relationships of uses and extend, in feature diagram relationships as in single adaptor, multiple adaptor, and options and in component and connector relationships such as the use of variants and options. The fourth criterion is on the specification of the variation points. Though it's not being shown in the case study, we have proposed the specification of the variation points at the requirements level which can be referred in (Halim, Jawawi et al. 2009). Nevertheless, specification of variation points at architectural level is yet to be defined. The following evaluation criteria is on case tool support. With the use of SysML profile which extends from UML itself, the notation can be used in any tools which support UML. Nonetheless, a fully automated tool is still being designed in order to automatically manage the variability of the models. The last evaluation criterion, unification in the proposed approach is achieved with the ability to transfer variability in models at both abstraction levels. At requirements level, variability information is transformed between use case, feature model and parametric diagram. The variabilities in both use case and feature model are then transferred to the component and connector model through decision model. Therefore, from the proposed mapping from each of the metamodels representing the use case, feature model, parametric model and component and connector model, an initial unified modeling of variability can be achieved.

Table 1 summarizes the discussion related to the first classification. Based on Table 1, the evaluation is done on our proposed notation only and there is no comparison done to other existing methods.

7. Conclusion

An initial mapping between multiple models at requirements level to an architectural model has been paved. The applicability of the approach has been validated in AMRPL case study. The proposed notations and annotation used to model the AMRPL have also been evaluated using an evaluation framework (Djebbi and Salinesi 2006). From the evaluation there are several criteria have been fulfilled by the proposed notation among them are its readability, simplicity and expressiveness, explicit variability types, specification for the variability, unified modeling and tool support. Nonetheless the mapping have not yet consider design decision as an intermediate model for vertical mapping between domain requirements to domain architecture. The initial mapping contain basically a syntactic information of how it can possibly be done. The semantics and rules of the mapping is the future work of this research as these two elements are important for a more consistent approach of multiple model mapping. In this paper also, an initial use of parametric model to represent quality requirements has been shown. While it shows significant new way of using parametric diagram which previously known to only represent mathematical equations, nonetheless further refinement of how the model can be used to show the affect of non functional requirements at architectural levels is strongly needed. The proposed approach of using lightweight mechanism in representing the extension to map and represent the models at different levels of abstraction also need to be evaluated with a proper matrix to ensure its quality in representing PL architecture. Therefore, our future work is on refining the design decision model and how the rules at requirements and architecture level can be implemented in the design decision as a mapping between both abstraction levels.

8. Acknowledgement

This research is fully funded by the Research University Grant (RUG) from the Universiti Teknologi Malaysia (UTM) and Ministry of Higher Education (MOHE) under Cost Center No.Q.J130000.7128.03J23. Our profound appreciation also goes to ERetSEL lab members for their continuous support in the working of this paper.

9. References

Armour, F., G. Miller, et al. (2001). Advanced use case modeling: software systems, Addison-Wesley.

Aurum, A. and C. Wohlin (2005). Engineering and managing software requirements, Springer Verlag.

Avgeriou, P., P. Kruchten, et al. (2007). Sharing and Reusing Architectural Knowledge--Architecture, Rationale, and Design Intent, IEEE Computer Society.

Bachmann, F. and L. Bass (2001). Managing Variability in Software Architectures. Proceedings of the 2001 Symposium on Software reusability: Putting Software Reuse in Context Toronto, Ontario, Canada, ACM Press.

Bachmann, F., L. Bass, et al. (2005). Designing software architectures to achieve quality attribute requirements, IET.

Bass, L., P. Clements, et al. (2003). Software architecture in practice, Addison-Wesley Longman Publishing Co., Inc.

Berg, K., J. Bishop, et al. (2005). Tracing Software Product Line Variability: from Problem to Solution Space. Proceedings of the 2005 annual research conference of the South African institute of computer scientists and information technologists on IT research in developing countries, White River, South Africa South African Institute for Computer Scientists and Information Technologists.

Bosch, J. (2000). Design and Use of Software Architectures: Adopting and Evolving a Product-Line Approach, Addison-Wesley.

Bosch, J. (2004). "Software architecture: The next step." Lecture notes in computer science: 194-199.

Bragança, A. and R. J. Machado (2009). "A model-driven approach for the derivation of architectural requirements of software product lines." Innovations in Systems and Software Engineering 5(1): 65-78.

Brown, T. J., R. Gawley, et al. (2006). Weaving behavior into feature models for embedded system families, Baltimore, MD, United states, Inst. of Elec. and Elec. Eng. Computer Society.

Brown, T. J., R. Gawley, et al. (2006). Weaving behavior into feature models for embedded system families.

Bühne, S., K. Lauenroth, et al. (2004). Why is it not Sufficient to Model Requirements Variability with Feature Models?

Capilla, R. and M. Ali Babar (2008). On the Role of Architectural Design Decisions in Software Product Line Engineering Software Architecture, Springer Berlin / Heidelberg. 5292: 241-255.

Chastek, G. (2001). Product Line Analysis: A Practical Introduction. Pittsburgh, Software Eng. Inst. (SEI), Carnegie Mellon Univ.

Clements, P., F. Bachmann, et al. (2003). Documenting software architectures: views and beyond, Addison-Wesley, Boston.

Dashofy, E. M., A. Hoek, et al. (2005). "A comprehensive approach for the development of modular software architecture description languages." ACM Transactions on Software Engineering and Methodology (TOSEM) 14(2): 199-245.

Dhungana, D. (2006). Integrated variability modeling of features and architecture in software product line engineering. 21st IEEE/ACM International Conference on Automated Software Engineering (ASE'06), Tokyo, Japan, Institute of Electrical and Electronics Engineers Computer Society, Piscataway, NJ 08855-1331, United States.

Dhungana, D., R. Rabiser, et al. (2007). "Decision-oriented modeling of product line architectures."

Friedenthal, S., A. Moore, et al. (2008). A Practical Guide to SysML: Systems Model Language, Morgan Kaufmann.

Garlan, D. (2000). "Software architecture: a roadmap." Proceedings of the Conference on The Future of Software Engineering: 91-101.

Gomaa, H. (2005). Designing Software Product Lines with UML. From use cases to pattern-based software Architectures, Addison Wesley.

Gomaa, H. and M. E. Shin (2008). "Multiple-view modelling and meta-modelling of software product lines."

Halim, S. A., D. N. A. Jawawi, et al. (2009). Requirements Identification and Representation in Software Product Line. Asia Pacific Software Engineering Conference (APSEC'09), Pulau Pinang, Malaysia, IEEE.

Holt, J. and S. Perry (2008). SysML for systems engineering, Institution of Engineering & Technology (IET).

Kaindl, H. and J. Falb (2008). Can We Transform Requirements into Architecture? International Conference on Software Engineering Advances (ICSEA'08) IEEE Computer Society.

Kandé, M. M. and A. Strohmeier (2000). Towards a UML profile for software architecture descriptions, Springer-Verlag.

Kircher, M., C. Schwanninger, et al. (2006). Transitioning to a software product family approach - challenges and best practices. Software Product Line Conference, 2006 10th International.

Lee, K. and K. C. Kang (2004). "Feature dependency analysis for product line component design." Software Reuse: Methods, Techniques and Tools: 69-85.

Liming, Z., M. A. Babar, et al. (2004). Mining patterns to support software architecture evaluation. Software Architecture, 2004. WICSA 2004. Proceedings. Fourth Working IEEE/IFIP Conference on.

Lin, Y., H. Ye, et al. (2010). An Approach for Modelling Software Product Line Architecture. International Conference on Computational Intelligence and Software Engineering (CiSE), Wuhan, China, IEEE.

Magnus, E., B. Jurgen, et al. (2009). "Managing requirements specifications for product lines - An approach and industry case study." J. Syst. Softw. 82(3): 435-447.

Mahvish, K. and G. Tony (2009). "A systematic review of domain analysis solutions for product lines." J. Syst. Softw. 82(12): 1982-2003.

Mannion, M. and H. Kaindl (2008). "Using parameters and discriminants for product line requirements." Systems Engineering 11(1).

Matinlassi, M. (2004). Comparison of Software Product Line Architecture Design Methods: COPA, FAST, FORM, KobrA and QADA. Proceedings of the International Conference on Software Engineering (ICSE'04), IEEE.

Medvidovic, N., E. M. Dashofy, et al. (2007). "Moving architectural description from under the technology lamppost." Information and Software Technology 49(1): 12-31.

Medvidovic, N., P. Grünbacher, et al. (2003). "Bridging models across the software lifecycle." Journal of Systems and Software 68(3): 199-215.

Medvidovic, N., D. S. Rosenblum, et al. (2002). "Modeling software architectures in the Unified Modeling Language." ACM Transactions on Software Engineering and Methodology (TOSEM) 11(1): 2-57.

Mikyeong, M., Y. Keunhyuk, et al. (2005). "An approach to developing domain requirements as a core asset based on commonality and variability analysis in a product line." Software Engineering, IEEE Transactions on 31(7): 551-569.

Moon, M., Yeom, K and Chae, HS (2005). "An Approach to Developing Domain Requirements as a Core Asset Based on Commonality and Variability Analysis in Product Line." IEEE Transactions on Software Engineering 31(7): 551-569.

Oquendo, F., B. Warboys, et al. (2004). Distilling Scenarios from Patterns for Software Architecture Evaluation – A Position Paper. Software Architecture, Springer Berlin / Heidelberg. 3047: 225-229.

Paech, B., A. H. Dutoit, et al. (2002). Functional requirements, non-functional requirements, and architecture should not be separated - A position paper. REFSQ, Essen.

Polzer, A., S. Kowalewski, et al. (2009). Applying Software Product Line Techniques in Model-based Embedded Systems Engineering. MOMPES 2009, Vancouver, Canada.

Savolainen, J., I. Oliver, et al. (2005). Transitioning from product line requirements to product line architecture, Edinburgh, Scotland, United Kingdom, Institute of Electrical and Electronics Engineers Computer Society, Piscataway, NJ 08855-1331, United States.

Savolainen, J., T. Vehkomäki, et al. (2002). "An Integrated Model for Requirements Structuring and Architecture Design." Proceedings of the Seventh Australian Workshop on Requirements Engineering, Melbourne.

Schmid, K. and I. John (2004). "A customizable approach to full lifecycle variability management." Science of Computer Programming 53(3): 259-284.

Sochos, P., M. Riebisch, et al. (2006). The Feature-Architecture Mapping (FArM) Method for Feature-Oriented Development of Software Product Lines. Proceedings of the 13th Annual IEEE International Symposium and Workshop on Engineering and Computer Based Systems (ECBS'06).

Taylor, R. N., N. Medvidovic, et al. (2009). "Software Architecture: Foundations, Theory, and Practice."

Thiel, S. and A. Hein (2002). Systematic Integration of Variability into Product Line Architecture Design. Software Product Lines : Second International Conference, SPLC 2, San Diego, CA, USA, August 19-22, 2002. Proceedings: 67-102.

Turban, B., M. Kucera, et al. (2009). Bridging the Requirements to Design Traceability Gap Intelligent Technical Systems, Springer Netherlands. 38: 275-288.

Yu, C. C., A. L. Akhihebbal, et al. (1998). Handling Variant Requirements in Software Architectures for Product Families. Proceedings of the Second International ESPRIT ARES Workshop on Development and Evolution of Software Architectures for Product Families, Springer-Verlag London, UK.

Zhang, W., H. Mei, et al. (2006). "Feature-driven requirement dependency analysis and high-level software design." Requirements Engineering 11(3): 205-220.

Zhu, C., L. Yuqin, et al. (2007). "A Feature Oriented Approach to Mapping from Domain Requirements to Product Line Architecture." Journal of Computer Research and Development 7.

Zhu, L. and I. Gorton (2007). Uml profiles for design decisions and non-functional requirements, IEEE Computer Society.

3

Transformational Variability Modeling Approach to Configurable Business System Application

Marcel Fouda Ndjodo[1] and Amougou Ngoumou[2]
[1]*University of Yaounde I*
[2]*University of Douala*
Cameroon

1. Introduction

For more than ten years now, adaptation of software systems has become a major challenge for the software engineering community which has proposed different reference architectures and systematic approaches to address this challenging research topic. In the literature, the concept of adaptability is very broad and has many unclear and inconsistent definitions, with many closed-related types of non functional requirements such as flexibility, evolvability, transformability, reusability, robustness, configurability, etc. (see (Subramanian & Chung, 2001a) for a sample of representative definitions). This broad nature of adaptability makes it critical in practice since one of the problems in dealing with it is to give a clear and non ambiguous definition of adaptation and adaptability.

This contribution is based on the intuitive definition of N. Subramanian and L. Chung who consider that "adaptation means change in the system to accommodate change in its environment", and "adaptability is the extent to which a system adapts to change in its environment" (Subramanian & Chung, 2001a, 2001b). Since we also agree with them that, "software architecture should itself be adaptable for the final software system to be adaptable", this chapter, which is a continuation of our earlier work on business component semantics (BCS) extension and transformation of feature-oriented models (Fouda & Amougou, 2009, 2010), describes an engineering approach to support adaptation at architectural level of enterprise systems.

The term enterprise system (ES) came into fashion somewhat recently, but the concept behind it has been subject to academic discussion for a long time now and has evolved from an historic development in Business, Computer Science, and Information Systems. Over the last years, ES have evolved to comprehensive IT-supported business solutions that presumptively support and enhance organizations in their operations. Often times, ES refer to the larger set of all large organization-wide packaged applications with a process orientation. They have to be configured to suit the requirements of an organization (alignment with organizational requirements). In order to facilitate the alignment process, most ES solutions provide reference models that describe the functionality and structure of the system. But, research shows that reference models still are only of limited use to the configuration process. According to M. Rosemanna and W.M.P. van der Aalst (Rosemanna

& van der Aalst, 2003), this is mainly due to a lack of conceptual support for configuration in the underlying modeling language. Following this line of argumentation, they have defined a language and a process for the design and usage of *configurable reference models* in a model-driven approach towards ES configuration (Recker et al., 2006).

Computer-based systems built using ES are types of information systems (IS) which, according to Jeffrey L. Whitten and al. (Whitten et al., 2001), are intrinsically linked to an organization (also referred to, hereafter, as an enterprise) because "an IS is an arrangement of persons, data, procedures and technology tools which interact to insure the collection, processing, storage and the diffusion of essential information to the life of an organization". Since each enterprise must be adapted permanently to the evolution of its environment, information systems are therefore intrinsically dynamic due to the fact that any adaptation of an enterprise to its moving environment triggers an information system change whose aim is to adapt the IS to its new environment.

A change in an IS, is any observable mutation and/or evolution of one or many of its building blocks: people, data, processes or interface (Whitten et al., 2001; Zachman, 1987). We qualify as "major" any change that results in a larger deviation of the information system definition. While robustness (i.e. the ability to tolerate some deviations in the environment) can be added to a software system at the design or even implementation stage, adaptability (i.e. the ability to adapt to larger deviations in the environment) cannot be added at such late stages. Adaptability can be enforced only if it is considered at the architecture development stage (Subramanian & Chung, 2001b). We go further in that direction by considering the IS architecture development stage, i.e. the enterprise process modeling, should be the initial stage where adaptability is taken in consideration.

Enterprise modeling (Bernus, 2003; Fox & Gruninger, 1998; Lankhorst, 2004; Vernadat, 2002) is a critical building block to establishing an agile, robust enterprise architecture that keeps pace with the fast moving business. It is the first building block in aligning the IT initiative with the business objectives. The aim of an enterprise model, named here "*business system architecture*" (BSA), is to bring together business operations and IT. The BSA serves as the foundation, framework and guidepost necessary to understand the enterprise and its environment.

The aim of this chapter is to propose and illustrate a reusable business component-based approach to develop BSAs with an innate potential to evolve and adapt to new requirements. To be more concise, the chapter's contribution is two-fold: First, it introduces an adaptable BSA modeling framework covering an architecture description language which formalizes the FORM engineering assets (Kang et al., 2002, 2003; Lee et al., 2000) as reusable business components (Ramadour & Cauvet, 2002) which provide domain knowledge reusable during IS engineering and a generic abstract model for adaptable business architectures. Second a transformational (Rotenstreich, 1992) engineering process for adaptable BSA design and use is given.

Our approach is an integrated system product line approach, like PLUSS+ (Eriksson et al., 2010), in the sense that it extends traditional systems engineering by incorporating ideas from software product line (SPL) engineering. It integrates a product line method managing variability with a software engineering methodology. It is based on the traditional *domain engineering-application engineering* view of software product line development (van der

Linden et al., 2007; Weiss & Lai, 1999). SPL engineering is a paradigm to develop software applications (software-intensive systems and software products) using platforms and mass customization (Pohl et al., 2005). Developing applications using platforms means to plan proactively for reuse, to build reusable parts, and to reuse what has been built for reuse. Building applications for mass customization means employing the concept of managed variability, i.e. the commonalities and differences in the applications (in terms of requirements, architecture, components, and test artifacts) of the product line have to be modeled.

The chapter is organized as follows: section 2 presents the modeling framework, section 3 then outlines the associated transformational engineering process, and section 4 concludes the chapter.

2. Modeling approach

This section outlines a generic conceptual framework for adaptable BSA. This framework is generic in the sense that it is not dependent on a specific modeling technique or method. However, a requirement for the application of our engineering process is that the engineering method used throughout the process must manage *variability* (Kang et al., 2010) in order to facilitate the derivation of model variants from the initial model. The main idea is to give *reusable business component* (Ramadour & Cauvet, 2002) semantics (rBCS) to the assets of a domain-specific architecture design method *M* by providing for each structure the context in which it can be reused. The resulting method, named *M/BCS* (read "M with business component semantics"), produces *M*-adaptable domain-specific architectures.

The model for adaptable BSA specification given in this section is based on a well established method in the product line engineering research community: the feature-oriented reuse method (FORM) (Kang et al., 1998).

2.1 Business component semantics

We use the model for conceptual business components specification of P. Ramadour and C. Cauvet (Ramadour & Cauvet, 2002) to define reusable domain-specific architecture assets. In this model, a business component integrates both reusable knowledge (object structures) and contextual knowledge guiding the reuse of the component. The context of a structure specifies specific requirements (set of constraints) accomplished by the structure and therefore indicates the suitable situation(s) in which a structure can be reused. The three levels of contextual constraints (business goals, business processes and business rules) considered by the model to specify conceptual business components clearly indicate that the conceptual business components of Ramadour and Cauvet are closely-related to enterprise process models assets (Bernus, 2003; Fox & Gruninger, 1998; Lankhorst, 2004; Vernadat, 2002). In this model, each business component has three constituents: a *name*, a *descriptor* and a *realization*:

- Descriptors explain when and why use components. A descriptor has an *intention* and a *context*. The intention is the expression of the generic modeling problem. The term "generic" here means that this problem does not refer to the context in which it is supposed to be solved. The context of a business component details its main business activity (*domain*) in terms of atomic and non atomic sub activities (*process*) and explains the choice of one alternative and not the other (*common, optional, variabilities*).

- Realizations provide solutions to the modeling problems expressed in the descriptor sections. Solutions are the reusable part of the business component; they may have adaptation points that are parameters whose values are fixed at the reuse moment.

We use the formal language Z to formalize this business component model in order to allow a rigorous study of its properties. Due to space constraints, this model cannot be given here. Figure 1, gives the specification skeleton, where $\mathbb{F}A$ denotes the set of finite subsets of *A* and *Class* is the set of classes of objects (as used in the object-oriented terminology). The detailed specification is given in (Fouda & Amougou, 2009).

BusinessComponent = =*[name:* ***Text;*** *descriptor:****Descriptor;*** *realization:* ***Realization*** */]*
Descriptor = = *[intention :* ***Intention*** *; context :* ***Context*** */]*
Intention = = *[action:* ***EnginneeringActivity;*** *target:* ***Interest*** */]*
Context = = *[domain :* ***Domain*** *; process :* $\mathbb{F}$ ***Context*** */]*
Realization = = *[solution:* ***Solution;*** *adaptationpoints :* ***AdaptationPoints*** */]*
Interest = ***Domain*** / ***BusinessObjects***
Domain = = *[action:* ***BusinessActivity;*** *target :* ***BusinessObjects*** */]*
BusinessActivity == *[common:* ***BusinessActivity*** *;*
optional: $\mathbb{F}$ ***BusinessActivity;***
variabilities: $\mathbb{F}$ $\mathbb{F}$ ***BusinessActivity***
atomic: ***Boolean*** */]*
BusinessObjects = = $\mathbb{F}$***Class***

Fig. 1. A formal specification of a business component

The types of solutions depend on the types of the business components. A solution can be a system decomposition, an activity organization or an object description, or anything else depending on the intention of the component. If this intention is to implement an activity of a product line engineering method (e.g. feature analysis), then the type of the solution is necessarily a kind of asset produced by the method (e.g. a feature model).

The BCS approach for adaptable business system architecture, which is advocated here, is a way to envelop assets of a product line engineering method with a domain knowledge layer. This layer, which indicates the purpose intended by the asset and the constraints it solve, provides the context in which it can be reused. It formally defines the extent to which the asset adapts to change in its environment. This additional layer is in fact an "adaptability information layer".

2.2 Business architecture description language

FORM/BCS architecture description language is specified through the description of its four main concepts: feature business components, subsystem architecture business components, process architecture business components, module business components and adaptable system architectures.

2.2.1 Feature business component

In FORM, a feature model of a domain gives the "intention" of that domain in terms of generic features which literally marks a distinct service, operation or function visible by users and application developers of the domain. FORM/BCS specifies a feature model of a domain as a business reusable component of that domain which captures the commonalities and differences of applications in that domain in terms of features (Figure 2).

The type *Feature* specifies business activities. A business activity is caused by an event which is applied to a target set of objects. Features have a generalization (in the sense of object-oriented analysis) and decomposition. A feature's decomposition gives the set of its common (sub) features which indicate reuse opportunity, the set of its optional (sub) features and the set of its groups of alternate (sub) features.

FeatureBusinessComponent *= = [name :**Name** ;*
*descriptor:**Descriptor**;*
*realization: **Realization***
fbc:FeatureBusinessComponent,
solution(realization(fbc)) ***Feature***
Adaptationpoints(realization(fbc)) *(Feature ×* ***Feature)]***

Feature *= =[activity: **BusinessActivity** ;*
*objects: **BusinessObjectst** ;*
decomposition:[common: ***Feature****; optional:* ***Feature****;*
variabilities: ***Feature****]*
generalization: ***Feature*** *]*

Fig. 2. The feature business component model

2.2.2 Subsystem architecture business component

A subsystem architecture business component (Figure 3) describes a system in terms of abstract high level subsystems and the relationships between them. Graphically, the solution of a subsystem architecture business component is represented as a symmetric boolean matrix in which rows and columns represent the different subsystems of the business component and the values of the matrix indicate the existence of links between these subsystems.

SubSystemBusinessComponent *= =*
[name: ***Name****; descriptor:* ***Descriptor****; realization:* ***Realization***
ssbc: SubSystemBusinessComponent ,
solution(realization(ssbc)) ***SubsystemArchitecture***
adapationpoints(realization(ssbc)) ***(SubSystem***× ***SubSystem)]***

SubsystemArchitecture *= =*
[subsystems: ***SubSystem*** *; Links:* ***(Subsystem SubSystem)*** *]*
SubSystem *=* ***Feature***

Fig. 3. The subsystem business component model

2.2.3 Process architecture business component

A process architecture business component represents a concurrency structure in terms of concurrent business activities to which functional elements are allocated; the deployment architecture shows an allocation of business activities to resources (Figure 4).

The type *ProcessArchitecture* specifies process architectures. A process architecture is a set of business activities (tasks) and classes of objects (data). Each business activity operates on a class of objects (data accesses) and business activities exchange messages between them in the form of actions call or with the environment (null).

ProcessBusinessComponent *= =*
[name: ***Name****; descriptor:****Descriptor****; realization:* ***Realization***
pbc:ProcessBusinessComponent,
solution(realization(pbc)) ***ProcessArchitecture***
adaptationpoints(realization(pbc))
(BusinessActivity× BusinessActivity)]

ProcessArchitecture *= =*
[tasks: ***BusinessActivity*** *;*
data : ***Class;***
dataaccess: [name: ***Name****; access:* ***BusinessActivity×Class*** *]*
messages: [name: ***Name****; call:* ***(BusinessActivity*** *{null}) ×*
(BusinessActivity *{null})]]*

Fig. 4. The process business component model

2.2.4 Module business component

Module business components are refinements of process business architecture components. A module business component may be associated with a set of relevant features. Also, alternative features may be implemented as a template module or a higher level module with an interface that could hide all the different alternatives (Figure 5).

ModuleBusinessComponent *= =*
[name: ***Name*** *; descriptor:****Descriptor****; realization:* ***Realization***
mbc:ModuleBusinessComponent,
solution(realization(mbc)) ***Module***
adaptationpoints(realization(mbc)) ***(Module× Module)]***

Module *= = [pseudonym :* ***Name*** *;*
parameters: ***Parameter;***
description: [task: ***BusinessActivity;***
included: ***Module;***
external: ***Module*** *]*
specification: ***PseudoCode*** *]*

Fig. 5. The module business component model

A business module has a name, a list of parameters, a code in a pseudo language and a description which defines the task done by the module and the modules required for its execution, some of them are included in the module and some others are external.

2.2.5 Adaptable system architecture

FORM-based adaptable business architectures (Figure 6) have four perspectives or views:

- The *service view*, which is a set of feature business components (the functional perspectives), provides the solution for the analysis of the service provided by a business organization.
- The *system view*, which is a set of subsystem business components (the structural perspectives), gives the solution for the decomposition of a business organization.
- The *process view*, which is a set of process business components (the procedural perspectives), provides the solution for the description of the processes of a business organization.
- The *logical view*, which is a set of module business components (the logical perspectives), gives the solution for the specification of application modules associated to sub processes or tasks of a business organization.

The reusable business components defining adaptable system architectures can be stored in a database which can be requested using engineering by reuse operators developed by P. Ramadour (Ramadour, 2001): search, selection, adaptation, and composition operators.

AdaptableArchitecture = = *[service View:* ***FunctionalPerspective****;*
systemView : ***StructuralPerspective****;*
processView: ***ProceduralPerspective****;*
logicalView: ***LogicalPerspective*** *];*
FunctionalPerspective = = *FeatureBusinessComponent;*
StructuralPerspective = = *SubsystemBusinessComponent;*
ProceduralPerspective = = *ProcessBusinessComponent;*
LogicalPerspective= = *ModuleBusinessComponent*

Fig. 6. The Adaptable business architecture model

3. Adaptable architectures engineering

In this section, we describe a system engineering methodology for the production and use of adaptable business architectures. Systems engineering focuses on stakeholder needs and the required functionality early in the development cycle to synthesize an overall system design that captures those requirements from a total life-cycle perspective. Our approach is an integrated system product line approach, like PLUSS+ (Eriksson et al., 2010), in the sense that it extends traditional systems engineering by incorporating ideas from software product line engineering. It integrates a product line method managing variability with a software engineering methodology. It is based on the traditional *domain engineering-application engineering* view of software product line development (van der Linden et al., 2007; Weiss & Lai, 1999).

The purpose of domain engineering is to develop a product line's reusable core assets to provide a production capability for products (Northrop, 2002) and the purpose of application engineering is to generate new systems utilizing the assets developed by domain engineering. We refer to the domain engineering activities of our methodology as *horizontal engineering process* and the application engineering activities as *vertical engineering process* to indicate that the purpose of application engineering is to refine business architectures at more low levels of abstraction (Figure 7).

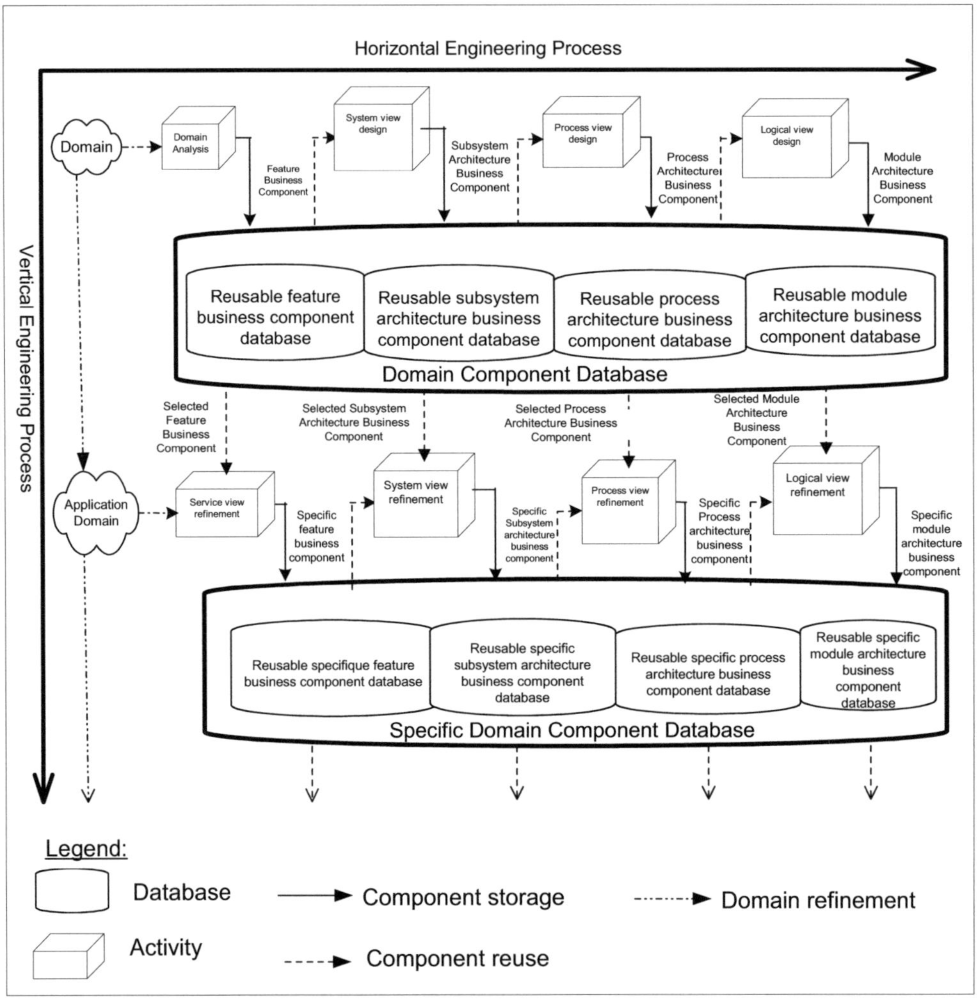

Fig. 7. The adaptable business architecture engineering process

The horizontal process, which corresponds to the "engineering for reuse" approach, gives the possibility to analyze a product line domain and develop adaptable architectures of that domain. These abstract reusable models can be refined ("engineering by reuse" approach) by the vertical engineering process in order to derive the specific business components of an application domain, which is to configure a suitable application from domain engineering.

3.1 Horizontal engineering process

The horizontal engineering process has been done in (Fouda & Amougou, 2010). It is a transformational method (Partsch, 1992; Rotenstreich, 1992), based on a set of provably semantics-preserving derivation rules called constructors.

The aim of a constructor is to transform, according to a formal rule called the construction schema, a kind of architectural artifact (the input type of the constructor) to another kind of architectural artifact (the output type of the constructor) by preserving all the system properties incorporated in any given input. The definition of a constructor therefore has three parts: the specification of the input type, the specification of the output type and, the specification of the construction rule which defines, through a construction schema and a set of semantics rules, how to build a semantics preserving output from a given input.

The horizontal engineering process has three constructors: the *system view constructor* which supports the system view design activity, the *process view constructor* which supports the process view design activity and the *logical view constructor* which support the logical view design activity. The service view of a system is the starting point of the process; this view is therefore obtained by applying any relevant requirement analysis technique.

3.1.1 System views design

The purpose of the system view design activity is to derive system views from service views. This activity is carried by the total function *SVC*, the system view constructor, whose purpose is to construct structural perspectives from functional perspectives of organizations. Figure 8, which intensively uses the adaptable business architecture model defined in section 2, specifies the system view constructor. In that figure, any text inside /* */ is a comment which explains the formal notation.

Input: A functional perspective *fp* of an organization.

Output: A structural perspective *SVC(fp)* of the organization.

Construction schema:

$$SVC\ (fp) = (SVC.name(fp),\ SVC.descriptor(fp),\ SVC.realization(fp))$$

Semantics rules:

1. *SVC.name(fp) = text*
   /* *text* is any text used by the designer to name the reusable business component modeling the structural perspective */
2. *SVC.descriptor(fp) = (SVC.intention(fp), SVC.context(fp))*
   2.1. $SVC.intention(fp) = <(decompose)_{ACTION}\ (domain(descriptor(fp))_{TARGET})>$,
   /* The intention of the structural perspective *SVC(fp)* is to decompose the business domain of *fp* */
   2.2. *SVC.context(fp) = context(descriptor(fp))*
   /* The context of *SVC (fp)* is the same as the context of *fp* */
3. *SVC.realization(fp) = (SVC.solution(fp), SVC.adaptation_points(fp))*
   3.1. *SVC.solution(fp) = (SVC.subsystems(fp), SVC.links(fp))*
   3.1.1. *SVC.subsystems(fp)* is the partition of the solution of the realization of *fp* defined as follows:
   3.1.1.1. $SVC.subsystems(fp) \subseteq \mathbb{F}\mathbb{F}\,Feature$
   3.1.1.2. $\cup(F \in SVC.subsystems(fp)) = decomposition(solution(realization(fp)))$
   3.1.1.3. $\forall F1, F2 \in SVC.subsystems(fp),\ F1 \neq F2 \Rightarrow F1 \cap F2 = \emptyset))$
   3.1.1.4. $\forall F \in SVC.subsystems(fp),\ \forall f \in Feature,\ \forall g \in Feature,$
   $((f \in F \wedge g \in F) \Leftrightarrow$
   $(\exists h \in F\ /\ (objects(f) \cap objects(h) \neq \emptyset) \wedge (objects(g) \cap objects(h) \neq \emptyset))).$

3.1.2. $SVC.links(fp) = \{(F,G) \in SVC.subsystems(fp) \times SVC.subsystems(fp) / \exists (f,g) \in F \times G \bullet decomposition(f) \cap decomposition(g) \neq \emptyset\}$

3.2. $SVC.adaptation\_points(fp) = \{(ss, subsystemrealizations(ss)) \bullet ss \in SVC.subsystems(fp) \wedge ss \cap adaptation\_points(realization(fp)) \neq \emptyset\}$

3.2.1. $subsystemrealizations(ss) = \{ss':Subsystem \bullet \forall f \in ss, \exists ! g \in ss' / g \in featurerealizations(f) \wedge \forall g \in ss', \exists f \in ss / g \in featurerealizations(f)\}$

3.2.2. $featurerealizations(f) = \{ g:Feature \bullet common(f) \subseteq common(g) \wedge \forall V \in variabilities(f), (\exists ! h \in common(g) \bullet h \in V) \wedge optional(g) \subseteq optional(f)\}$

Fig. 8. The system view construction rule

3.1.2 Process view design

The purpose of the process view design activity is to derive process views from system views of organizations. This activity is carried by the total function *PVC*, the process view constructor, whose purpose is to construct procedural perspectives from structural perspectives of organizations. Figure 9 defines the process view constructor.

Input: A structural perspective *sp* of an organization.

Output: A set of procedural perspectives *PVC(sp)* of the organization.

Construction schema:

$PVC(sp) = \{(PVC.name(p), PVC.descriptor(p), PVC.realization(p)) \bullet p \in process(sp)\}$

Semantics rules:

1. $PVC.name(p) = text$.
   /* *text* is any text used by the designer to name the reusable business component modeling the procedural perspective */
2. $PVC.descriptor(p) = (PVC.intention(p), PVC.context(p))$
   2.1. $PVC.intention(p) = (describe)_{ACTION}\ (p)_{TARGET}$
   /* The intention of the process architecture built from $p \in process(sp)$ is to describe p */
   2.2. $PVC.context(p) = (domain(sp), \{p\})$
   /* The business activity of the process architecture constructed from the process $p \in process\ (sp)$ is the same as the main activity of *sp* and it has only one sub activity p */
3. $PVC.realization(p) = (PVC.solution(p), PVC.adaptation\_points(p))$
   3.1. $PVC.solution(p) = (PVC.tasks(p), PVC.datas(p), PVC.dataaccess(p), PVC.messages(p))$
   3.1.1. $PVC.tasks(p) = decomposition(action(domain(p)))$
   /* Tasks of the process architecture constructed from $p \in process\ (sp)$ are obtained by decomposing the action of the domain of p */
   3.1.2. $PVC.data(p) = target(domain(p))$
   /* The data of the process architecture constructed from $p \in process(sp)$ are the business objects of the target of the domain of p */
   3.1.3. $PVC.dataaccess(p) = \{(t, c) \in decomposition(action(domain(p))) \times target(domain(p)) / decomposition(t) \cap operations(c) \neq \emptyset\}$
   /* The task *t* of the process architecture constructed from $p \in process\ (sp)$ can operate on a class of object *c* only if some subtasks of *t* are operations

of the class *c* */

3.1.4. *PVC.messages(p)* = *{(t1, t2)* ∈ *(decomposition (action(domain(p))))* ^{2} /
decomposition (t1) ∩ *decomposition (t2)* ≠∅*}*
/* Two tasks *t1* and t2 of the process architecture constructed from *p* ∈ *process (sp)* can exchange messages only if some subtasks of *t1* are subtasks *t2* */

3.1.5. *PVC.adaptation_points(p))* = *{(t1, A)* • *t1* ∈ *PVC.tasks(p)* ∧ *A* = *{t2 : BusinessActivity* • *common(t1)* ⊆ *common(t2)* ∧(∀ *V* ∈ *variabilities(t1),* ∃ *!g* ∈ *common(t2)* • *g* ∈ *V)* ∧
optional(t1) ⊆ *optional(t2)}* ∧ #*A* > 1*}*
/* Adaptation points of the process architecture constructed from *p* in *process(sp)* are tasks of the process architecture for which we have more than one realization */

Fig. 9. The process view construction rule

3.1.3 Logical view design

The purpose of the logical view design activity is to derive logical views from process views. This activity is carried by the total function *LVC*, the logical view constructor, whose purpose is to derive logical perspectives from procedural perspectives of organizations. Figure 10 defines the logical view constructor.

Input: A procedural perspective *pp* of an organization.

Output: A set of logical perspectives *LVC(pp)* of the organization.

Construction schema:
LVC.descriptor(t), LVC.realization(t)) •
t ∈ *process(p), p* ∈ *process(pp)}*

Semantics rules:

1. *LVC.name (t) = text*
/* *text* is any text used by the designer to name the reusable business component modeling the logical perspective */
2. *LVC.descriptor(t)* = *(LVC.intention(t), LVC.context(t))*
   2.1. *LVC.intention(t)* = <$(implement)_{ACTION}$ $(t)_{TARGET}$>
   /* The intention of the module architecture built from a task *t* ∈ *process(p)* and *p* ∈ *process(pp)*, is to implement *t* */
   2.2. *LVC.context(t)* = *(domain(pp), {t})*
3. *LVC.realization(t)* = *(LVC.solution(t), LVC.adaptation_points(t))*
   3.1. *LVC.solution(t)* = *(LVC. pseudonym (t), LVC.parameters(t), LVC.task(t), LVC.included(t),), LVC.external(t), LVC.specification(t))*
      3.1.1. *LVC. pseudonym (t) = text'*
      /* *text'* is any text used by the designer to name the solution of the module architecture component constructed from the task *t* ∈ *process(p)*, for any *p* ∈ *process(pp)* */
      3.1.2. *LVC.parameters(t)* is a set of business objects of the domain of *t*.
      3.1.3. *LVC.task(t)* = *action(domain(t))*
      /* The task of the solution of the module architecture constructed from

the context *t* is the action of the domain of *t* */

3.1.4. *LVC.included(t)* = $\{m{:}Module \bullet task(m) \in decomposition(action(domain(t))) \wedge specification(m) \neq \text{""}\}$

/* Modules included in the module architecture constructed from the context *t* are modules for which the task is a subtask of *t* and the specification is not empty*/

3.1.5. *LVC.external(t)* = $\{m{:}Module \bullet task(m) \in decomposition(action(domain(t))) \wedge specification(m) = \text{""}\}$

/* External modules in the module architecture constructed from the context *t* are module for which the task is a subtask of *t* and the specification is empty */

3.1.6. *LVC.specification(t)* = $\{specification(m) \bullet m \in LVC.included(t) \cup LVC.required(t)\}$

/* The specification of the module architecture constructed from the context *t* is the set of specifications of subtasks of t */

3.2. *LVC.adaptation_points(t)* = $\{(m1, A) \bullet m1 \in LVC.included(t) \wedge A = \{m2 : Module \bullet common(task(m1)) \subseteq common(task(m2)) \wedge (\forall V \in variabilities(task(m1)), \exists ! g \in common(task(m2)) \bullet g \in V) \wedge optional(task(m1)) \subseteq optional(task(2))\} \wedge \#A > 1\}$

/* Adaptation points of the module architecture of a context *t* are modules included in the module architecture of *t* for which we have more than one realization */

Fig. 10. The logical view construction rule

3.2 Vertical engineering process

The purpose of the vertical engineering process is to generate new systems utilizing the assets developed by horizontal engineering. Its ultimate goal is to configure a suitable business application from domain engineering. It refines architectural assets of a domain to low level assets of an application domain of that domain. This engineering process is also a transformational method based on a set of provably semantics-preserving refinement rules called refiners. The process has four refiners: the service view refiner which supports the service view refinement activity, the system view refiner which supports the system view refinement activity, the process view refiner which support the process view refinement activity and the logical view refiner which supports the logical view refinement activity (see Figure 7).

3.2.1 Service view refinement

The purpose of the service view refinement activity is to derive a service view of an application domain of a domain from the service view of that domain. This activity is carried by a total function *FMR*, the functional model refiner, defines in Figure 12, which refines feature business components, i.e. functional perspectives, of a domain to specific business components of an application domain by using decompositions of non atomic services of input feature business components. A service view refinement is triggered by a decomposition of an abstract service of the service view. Any decomposition defines an application domain since it specifies a specific manner to implement the service. Decompositions define how abstract (common and optional) services of domains are implemented in application domains.

Figure 11 shows an example of a decomposition of an abstract service (career management of state personnel governed by the general status of the public service or the labor code: C_{11}) of the Cameroon civil servant management information system which has been used as a case study for the method (Atsa et al., 2010). In this decomposition, the abstract service C_{11} is implemented only by four common actions; one of these actions (the recruitment process: C_{111}) is itself decomposed in four optional actions.

common(C_{11}) = { C_{111} = *(recruit = [{}, {absorb by qualification, absorb by competitive examination, contractualize, engage}, {}}])*$_{ACTION}$*(candidates, applications, competitive examinations, civil servants governed by the general status or the labor code, decisions)*$_{TARGET}$*(If the candidate has succeeded a competitive examination or has obtained a diploma giving the right to absorption or the Presidency of the Republic has given the authorization)*$_{DETAIL}$

C_{112} = *(advance)*$_{ACTION}$ *(applications, civil servants governed by the general status or the labor code, decisions)* $_{TARGET}$

C_{113} = *(liquidate)* $_{ACTION}$ *(applications, civil servants governed by the general status or the labor code, decisions)* $_{TARGET}$

C_{114} = *(transfer)* $_{ACTION}$ *(civil servants governed by the general status or the labor code, decisions)* $_{TARGET}$ }

optional(C_{11}) = {}
variabilities(C_{11}) = {}

Fig. 11. Decomposition of the non atomic service C_{11}

The refinement of a service view (see Figure 12 for the formal definition) replaces the decomposed service by its decomposition and integrates the new variability constraints in the new model.

Input: - A functional perspective *fp* of an organization - A decomposition *D* of an abstract service *s* of *fp*
Output: A specific functional perspective *FMR(fp,D)* of an application domain
Construction schema: *FMR (fp,D)= (FMR.name(fp,D), FMR.descriptor(fp,D), FMR.realization(fp,D))*
Semantics rules: **1.** *FMR.name(fp,D) = name(fp)* 2. *FMR.descriptor(fp,D) = (FMR.intention(fp,D), FMR.context(fp,D))* 2.1. *FMR.intention(fp,D) = intention(descriptor(fp))* 2.2. *FMR.context(fp,D) = (FMR.domain(fp,D), FMR.process(fp,D))* 2.2.1. *FMR.domain(fp,D) = domain(context(descriptor(fp)))* 2.2.2. *FMR.process(fp,D)* = $\{(f, \varnothing) \bullet f \in D\}$ **if** *process(context(descriptor(fp)))* = $\varnothing$ /* In this case, *s* is the main activity of *fp* and *D* defines its sub activities */ **and** *FMR.process(fp,D) = process(context(descriptor(fp)))* **if** *process(context(descriptor(fp)))* $\neq \varnothing$. /* A refinement of a sub activity of *fp* doesn't change the context of *fp* */

3. *FMR.realization(fp,D) = (FMR .solution(fp,D), FMR. adaptation_ points (fp,D))*
   3.1. *FMR.solution(fp,D) = solution(realization(fp)) • decomposition(s) =D*
/* *D* is the decomposition of the service *s* in the solution of the new business component */
   3.2. *FMR. adaptation _points (fp,D) = adaptationpoints (realization(fp))*
      if *(optional(D)* = ∅ ∧ *variabilities(D)* = ∅)
   /* The set of adaptation points of *fp* doesn't change if *D* decomposes *s* only in common sub services */
and
FMR. adaptation _points (fp,D) = adaptationpoints (realization(fp)) ∪
   {(s,variants(s,D))}
   if *optional(D)* ≠ ∅ ∨ *variabilities(D)* ≠ ∅
/* A new adaptation point based on the variants of *s* induced by the decomposition *D* is created if *D* defines optional or variable subservices of *s* */

Fig. 12. The service view refinement rule

Figure 14 shows the result of the refinement of the service view of the civil servant management information system (Figure 13) based on the decomposition given in Figure 11.

Name *:Functional model of the Cameroonian civil servant management information system*
Descriptor *:*
Intention *:(Analyze)*$_{ACTION}$*((manage)*$_{ACTION}$*(State personals and salaries)*$_{TARGET}$*)*$_{TARGET}$
Context *:*
Domain : C = (manage)$_{ACTION}$*(career, salaries, training, network, mail, system)*$_{TARGET}$
Process : C_1 *= (manage)*$_{ACTION}$*(civil servants career)*$_{TARGET}$
C_2 *= (manage)*$_{ACTION}$*(salaries)*$_{TARGET}$
C_3 *= (manage)*$_{ACTION}$*(training)*$_{TARGET}$
C_4 *= (manage)*$_{ACTION}$*(attributions)*$_{TARGET}$
C_5 *= (manage)*$_{ACTION}$*(mail)*$_{TARGET}$
/ sub-process of* C_1 **/*
C_{11} *= (manage)*$_{ACTION}$*(decisions, personnels governed by the general status or the labor code)*$_{TARGET}$
C_{12} *= (manage)*$_{ACTION}$*(decisions, magistrates)*$_{TARGET}$
C_{13} *= (manage)*$_{ACTION}$*(decisions, university lecturers)*$_{TARGET}$
C_{14} *= (manage)*$_{ACTION}$*(decisions, police officers)*$_{TARGET}$
C_{15} *= (transfer)*$_{ACTION}$*(decisions)*$_{TARGET}$
/ sub-process of* C_2 **/*
C_{21} *= (transfer)*$_{ACTION}$*(decisions)*$_{TARGET}$
C_{22} *= (calculate)*$_{ACTION}$*(salaries)*$_{TARGET}$
C_{23} *= (manage)*$_{ACTION}$*(workstation)*$_{TARGET}$
C_{24} *= (manage)*$_{ACTION}$*(profiles, workstations)*$_{TARGET}$
C_{25} *= (manage)*$_{ACTION}$*(connections, workstations)*$_{TARGET}$
/ sub-process of* C_4 **/*
C_{41} *= (manage)*$_{ACTION}$*(workstations)*$_{TARGET}$
C_{42} *= (manage)*$_{ACTION}$*(profiles, workstations)*$_{TARGET}$
C_{43} *= (manage)*$_{ACTION}$*(connections, workstations)*$_{TARGET}$
C_{44} *= (manage)*$_{ACTION}$*(transactions, workstations)*$_{TARGET}$

Realization :

Solution :

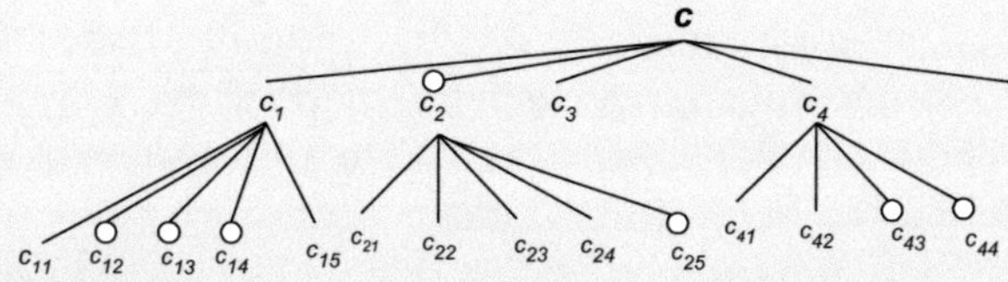

Adaptation points : {

(c, {{c_1, c_3, c_4, c_5}, {c1, c_2, c_3, c_4, c_5}}),

(c_1, {{c_{11}, c_{15}}, {c_{11}, c_{15}, c_{12}}, {c_{11}, c_{15}, c_{13}}, {c_{11}, c_{15}, c_{14}}, {c_{11}, c_{12}, c_{13}, c_{15}}, {c_{11}, c_{13}, c_{14}, c_{15}}, {c_{11}, c_{12}, c_{14}, c_{15}} et {c_{11}, c_{12}, c_{13}, c_{14}, c_{15}}}),

(c_2, {{c_{21}, c_{22}, c_{23}, c_{24}}, {c_{21}, c_{22}, c_{23}, c_{24}, c_{25}}}),

(c_4, {{c_{41}, c_{42}}, {c_{41}, c_{42}, c_{43}},{c_{41}, c_{42}, c_{44}},{ c_{41}, c_{42}, c_{43}, c_{44}}})

}

Fig. 13. Service view of Cameroon civil servant management IS

...

/ sub-process of C_{11} */*

C_{111} = *(recruit = [{}, {absorb by qualification, absorb by competitive examination, contractualize, engage}, {}}])*$_{ACTION}$*(candidates, applications, competitive examinations, civil servants governed by the general status or the labor code, decisions)*$_{TARGET}$*(If the candidate has succeeded a competitive examination or has obtained a diploma giving the right to absorption or the Presidency of the Republic has given the authorization)*$_{DETAIL}$

C_{112} = *(advance)*$_{ACTION}$ *(applications, civil servants governed by the general status or the labor code, decisions)* $_{TARGET}$

C_{113} = *(liquidate)* $_{ACTION}$ *(applications, civil servants governed by the general status or the labor code, decisions)* $_{TARGET}$

C_{114} = *(transfer)* $_{ACTION}$ *(civil servants governed by the general status or the labor code, decisions)* $_{TARGET}$

...

Realization :

Solution :

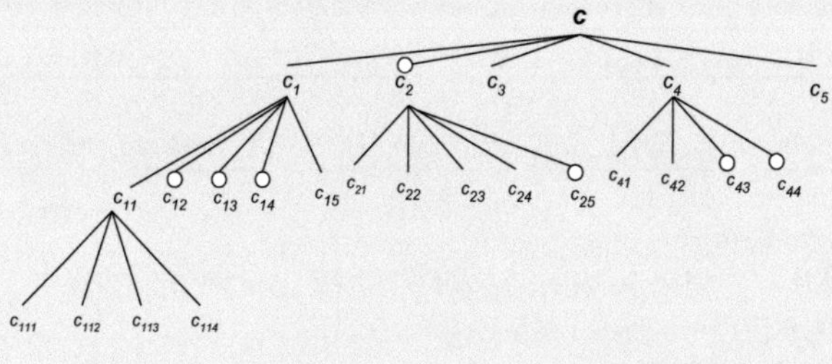

...

Fig. 14. A refined service view of Cameroon civil servant management IS

3.2.2 System view refinement

The purpose of the system view refinement activity is to derive a system view of an application domain of a domain from the system view of that domain. This activity is carried by a total function *SMR*, the structural model refiner, defines in figure 16, which refines subsystem business components, i.e. structural perspectives, of a domain to specific business components of an application domain by using decompositions of non atomic services in subsystems of input subsystem business components. A system view refinement is triggered by a decomposition of an abstract service in a subsystem of the subsystem view. Any decomposition defines an application domain since it specifies a specific manner to implement the service. Decompositions define how abstract services of domains are implemented in application domains. Figure 15 shows an example of a decomposition of an abstract service (career management of state personnels: C_1) of the Cameroon civil servant management information system.

$common(C_1) = \{C_{11} = (manage)_{ACTION}(decisions,\ personnels\ governed\ by\ the\ general\ status\ or\ the\ labor\ code)_{TARGET}\}$

$optional(C_1) = \{ C_{12} = (manage)_{ACTION}(decisions,\ magistrates)_{TARGET},$
$C_{13} = (manage)_{ACTION}(decisions,\ univerties's\ lecturers)_{TARGET},$
$C_{14} = (manage)_{ACTION}(decisions,\ police\ officers)_{TARGET},$
$C_{15} = (transfer)_{ACTION}(decisions)_{TARGET}\}$
$variabilities(C_1) = \{\}$

Fig. 15. Decomposition of the non atomic service C_1

In this decomposition, the abstract service C_1 is implemented by one common action and four optional actions.

The refinement of a system view (see Figure 16 for the formal definition) replaces the decomposed service by its decomposition and integrates the new variability constraints in the new model.

Input:
- A structural perspective *sp* of an organization,
- A decomposition *D* of a non atomic service *c* in a subsystem *ss* of *sp*.

Output: A specific system view perspective *SMR(sp,D)* of an application domain

Construction schema:
SMR (sp,D)= (SMR .name(sp,D), SMR .descriptor(sp,D), SMR .realization(sp,D))

Semantics rules:

1. *SMR .name(sp,D) = name(sp)*
2. *SMR .descriptor(sp,D) = (SMR .intention(sp,D), SMR .context(sp,D))*
   2.1. *SMR .intention(sp,D) = intention(descriptor(sp))*
   2.2. *SMR .context(sp,D) = (SMR .domain(sp, D), SMR .process(sp,D))*
      2.2.1. *SMR .domain(sp,D) = domain(context(descriptor(sp)))*
      2.2.2. $SMR\ .process(sp,D) = \{(f, \varnothing) \bullet f \in D\}$
      if $process(context(descriptor(sp))) = \varnothing$
      and
      SMR .process(sp,D) = process(context(descriptor(sp)))
      if $process(context(descriptor(sp))) \neq \varnothing$

3. $SMR.realization(sp,D) = (SMR.solution(sp,D), SMR.adaptation\_points(sp,D))$
3.1. $SMR.solution(sp,D) = (SMR.subsystems(sp,D), SMR.links(sp, D))$
3.1.1. $SMR.subsystems(sp,D) = subsystems(solution(realization(sp)))$
/* A system view refinement of a system doesn't change its subsystems */
3.1.2. $SMR.links(sp,D) = links(solution(realization(sp))) \cup \{(ss, t), t \in subsystems(solution(realization(sp))) \bullet \exists g \in t, D \cap decomposition(g) \neq \emptyset\}$
/* A refinement of the subsystem *ss* triggered by the decomposition *D* creates a new link between *ss* and any other subsystem which is not disjoint with *D* */
3.3. $SMR.adaptation\_points(sp,D) = adaptationpoints(realization(sp))$ **if** $(optional(D) = \emptyset \wedge variabilities(D) = \emptyset)$
/* The set of adaptation points of *sp* doesn't change if *D* decomposes *c* only in common sub services */
and
$SMR.adaptation\_points(sp,D) = adaptationpoints(realization(sp)) \cup \{(ss, variants(ss,D))\}$ **if** $optional(D) \neq \emptyset \vee variabilities(D) \neq \emptyset$
/* A new adaptation point based on the variants of *ss* induced by the decomposition *D* is created if *D* defines optional or variable subservices of *c* */

Fig. 16. The system view refinement rule

Figure 18 shows the result of the refinement of the system view of the civil servant management information system (Figure 17) based on the decomposition of Figure 15.

Name *:Structural Model of the Cameroonian civil servant management information system*
Descriptor *:*
Intention *:(Decompose)$_{ACTION}$((manage)$_{ACTION}$(career, salaries, training, natwork, mail, system)$_{TARGET}$)$_{TARGET}$*
Context *:*
Domain : C = (manage)$_{ACTION}$(career, salaries, training, network, mail, system)$_{TARGET}$
Process : C_1 = (manage)$_{ACTION}$(career)$_{TARGET}$
C_2 = (manage)$_{ACTION}$(salaries)$_{TARGET}$
C_3 = (manage)$_{ACTION}$(training)$_{TARGET}$
C_4 = (manage)$_{ACTION}$(attributions)$_{TARGET}$
C_5 = (manage)$_{ACTION}$(mail)$_{TARGET}$
/ sub-process of C2 */*
C_{21} = (transfer)$_{ACTION}$(decisions)$_{TARGET}$
C_{22} = (calculate)$_{ACTION}$(salaries)$_{TARGET}$
C_{23} = (manage)$_{ACTION}$(workstation)$_{TARGET}$
C_{24} = (manage)$_{ACTION}$(profiles, workstations)$_{TARGET}$
C_{25} = (manage)$_{ACTION}$(connections, workstations)$_{TARGET}$
/ sub-process of C4 */*
C_{41} = (manage)$_{ACTION}$(workstations)$_{TARGET}$
C_{42} = (manage)$_{ACTION}$(profiles, workstations)$_{TARGET}$
C_{43} = (manage)$_{ACTION}$(connections, workstations)$_{TARGET}$
C_{44} = (manage)$_{ACTION}$(transactions, workstations)$_{TARGET}$
...

Realization :
  Solution:
    Sub-systems: $\{SS_1 = \{c_1\}, SS_2 = \{c_2\}, SS_3 = \{c_3\}, SS_4 = \{c_4\}, SS_5 = \{c_5\}\}$
    Links: $\{SS_2 \leftrightarrow SS_5\}$
  Adaptation points: {
    $(SS_2, \{\{c_{21}, c_{22}, c_{23}, c_{24}\}, \{c_{21}, c_{22}, c_{23}, c_{24}, c_{25}\}\}),$
    $(SS_4, \{\{c_{41}, c_{42}\}, \{c_{41}, c_{42}, c_{43}\},\{c_{41}, c_{42}, c_{44}\},\{ c_{41}, c_{42}, c_{43}, c_{44}\}\})$
    }

Fig. 17. A system view of Cameroon civil servant management IS

...
/* *sous-processus de* C_1 */
C_{11} = *(manage)*$_{ACTION}$*(decisions, personals governed by the general status or the labor code)*$_{TARGET}$
C_{12} = *(manage)*$_{ACTION}$*(decisions, magistrates)*$_{TARGET}$
C_{13} = *(manage)*$_{ACTION}$*(decisions, universities's lecturers)*$_{TARGET}$
C_{14} = *(manage)*$_{ACTION}$*(decisions, police officers)*$_{TARGET}$
C_{15} = *(transfer)*$_{ACTION}$*(decisions)*$_{TARGET}$
...
Liens: $\{SS_1 \leftrightarrow SS_2, SS_2 \leftrightarrow SS_4\}$
Adaptation points: {
$(SS_1, \{\{c_{11}, c_{15}\}, \{c_{11}, c_{15}, c_{12}\}, \{c_{11}, c_{15}, c_{13}\}, \{c_{11}, c_{15}, c_{14}\}, \{c_{11}, c_{12}, c_{13}, c_{15}\}, \{c_{11}, c_{13}, c_{14}, c_{15}\}, \{c_{11}, c_{12}, c_{14}, c_{15}\}, \{c_{11}, c_{12}, c_{13}, c_{14}, c_{15}\}\}),$
$(SS_2, \{\{c_{21}, c_{22}, c_{23}, c_{24}\}, \{c_{21}, c_{22}, c_{23}, c_{24}, c_{25}\}\}),$
$(SS_4, \{\{c_{41}, c_{42}\}, \{c_{41}, c_{42}, c_{43}\},\{c_{41}, c_{42}, c_{44}\},\{ c_{41}, c_{42}, c_{43}, c_{44}\}\})$
}

Fig. 18. A refined system view of Cameroon civil servant management IS

3.2.3 Process view refinement

The purpose of the process view refinement activity is to derive a process view of an application domain of a domain from the process view of that domain. This activity is carried by a total function *PMR*, the procedural model refiner, defines in Figure 20, which refines process business components of a domain to specific business components of an application domain by using decompositions of non atomic tasks of input process business components. A process view refinement is triggered by a decomposition of a task of the process view. Any decomposition defines an application domain since it indicates a specific manner to implement the task. Decompositions define how abstract tasks of domains are implemented in application domains. Figure 19 shows an example of a decomposition of an abstract task (recruitment of state personnels governed by the general status of the public service or the labor code: C_{111}, see Figure 11) of the Cameroon civil servant management information system.

recruit = [{}, {absorb by qualification, absorb by competitive examination, contractualize, engage}, {}}]

Fig. 19. Decomposition of the non atomic service C_{111}

In this decomposition, the abstract task of C_{111} is implemented by four optional tasks.

The refinement of a process view (see Figure 20 for the formal definition) replaces the decomposed task by its decomposition and integrates the new variability constraints in the new model.

Input: - A procedural perspective *pp* of an organization, - A decomposition *D* of a non atomic task *t* of *pp*.
Output: A specific procedural perspective *PMR(pp,D)* of an application domain
Construction schema: *PMR (pp,D)= (PMR .name(pp,D), PMR .descriptor(pp,D), PMR .realization(pp,D))*
Semantics rules: **1.** *PMR .name(pp,D) = name(pp)* 2. *PMR .descriptor(pp,D) = descriptor(pp)* 3. *PMR .realization(pp, D) = (PMR .solution(pp,D), PMR . adaptation _points (pp,D))* 3.1. *PMR .solution(pp, D) = (PMR .tasks(pp,D), PMR .datas(pp,D), PMR .datasaccess(pp,D), PMR .messages(pp,D))* 3.1.1. *PMR .tasks(pp,D) = tasks (solution(realization(pp)))* 3.1.2. *PMR .data(pp,D) = data(solution(realization(pp)))* 3.1.3. *PMR .dataaccess(pp,D) = dataaccess(solution(realization(pp))) \ {(t, c)• ∃ u ∈ tasks(solution(realization(pp))), (u, c) ∈ datasaccess(solution(realization(pp))) ∧ D ∩ decomposition (u) ≠ ∅}* 3.1.4. *PMR .messages(pp,D) = messages(solution(realization(pp))) ∪ {(t, u) • D ∩ decomposition (u) ≠ ∅}* 3.2. *PMR. Adaptation_ points (pp,D) = adaptationpoints (realization(pp))* **if** *(optional(D) = ∅ ∧ variabilities(D) = ∅)* **and** *PMR .adaptation_points(pp,D) = adaptationpoints (realization(pbc)) ∪ {(t, variants(t,D))}* **if** *optional(D) ≠ ∅ ∨ variabilities(D) ≠ ∅*

Fig. 20. The process view refinement rule

Figure 22 shows the result of the refinement of the process view of the civil servant management information system (Figure 21) based on the decomposition of Figure 19.

Name: *Procedural model of career management of personals governed by the general status or the labor code in the Cameroonian civil servant management information system.* ***Descriptor*** *:* ***Intention*** *: (describe)$_{ACTION}$((manage = [{recruit, advance, liquidate, transfer}, {}, {}])$_{ACTION}$(candidates, applications, competitive examinations, civil servants governed by the general status or the labor code, decisions)$_{TARGET}$)$_{TARGET}$* ***Context*** *:* *Domain : C = (manage)$_{ACTION}$(career, salaries, training, network, mail, system)$_{TARGET}$* *Process : C_{11} = (manage = [{recruit, advance, liquidate, transfer}, {},*

{}])_{ACTION}(candidates, applications, competitive examinations, civil servants governed by the general status or the labor code, decisions)_{TARGET}
/ sub process of the process C_{11}*/*
C_{111} = (recruit)$_{ACTION}$(candidates, applications, competitive examinations, civil servants governed by the general status or the labor code, decisions)$_{TARGET}$(If the candidate has succeeded a competitive examination or has obtained a diploma giving the right to absorption or the Presidency of the Republic has given the authorization)$_{DETAIL}$
C_{112} = (advance)$_{ACTION}$ (applications, civil servants governed by the general status or the labor code, decisions) $_{TARGET}$
C_{113} = (liquidate) $_{ACTION}$ (applications, civil servants governed by the general status or the labor code, decisions) $_{TARGET}$
...

Realization :
Solution :
tasks: decomposition(action(C_{11}))
data: target(C_{11})
dataaccess: {(t, c) $\in$ decomposition(action(C_{11})) × target(C_{11}) / decomposition(t) $\cap$ operations(c) $\neq \emptyset$}
messages: {(t1, t2) $\in$ decomposition (action(C_{11})) × decomposition (action(C_{11})) / decomposition (t1) $\cap$ decomposition (t2) $\neq \emptyset$}
Adaptation points: {}

Fig. 21. A prrocess view of Cameroon civil servant management IS

Process :
...
C_{111} = (recruit = [{}, {absorb by qualification, absorb by competitive examination, contractualize, engage}, {}}])$_{ACTION}$(candidates, applications, competitive examinations, civil servants governed by the general status or the labor code, decisions)$_{TARGET}$(If the candidate has succeeded a competitive examination or has obtained a diploma giving the right to absorption or the Presidency of the Republic has given the authorization)$_{DETAIL}$
...

Realization :
Solution :
...
Adaptation points:
{(recruit, {{absorb by qualification}, {absorb by competitive examination}, {contractualize}, {engage}, { absorb by qualification, absorb by competitive examination }, { absorb by qualification, contractualize}, { absorb by qualification, engage}, {absorb by competitive examination, contractualize}, { absorb by competitive examination, engage}, {contractualize, engage},{ absorb by qualification, absorb by competitive examination, contractualize}, { absorb by qualification, absorb by competitive examination, engage}, { absorb by competitive examination, contractualize, engage}, { absorb by qualification, contractualize, engage}, { absorb by qualification, absorb by competitive examination, contractualize, engage}}) }

Fig. 22. A refined process view of Cameroon civil servant management IS

3.2.4 Logical view refinement

The purpose of the logical view refinement activity is to derive a logical view of an application domain of a domain from the logical view of that domain. This activity is carried by a total function *LMR*, the logical model refiner, defines in Figure 24, which refines module business components of a domain to specific business components of an application domain by using decompositions of non atomic business activities of input module business components.

A logical view refinement is triggered by a decomposition of a business activity of the logical view. Any decomposition defines an application domain since it specifies a specific manner to implement the business activity. Decompositions define how (common business activities, optional business activities, variability) abstract business activities of domains are implemented in application domains. Figure 23 shows example of a decomposition of an abstract business activity (absorption by qualification belonging to *optional(action* (C_{111})*)*) of the Cameroon civil servant management information system.

absorb by qualification = [{}, {prepare = [{initiate, validate, append visa, remove validation, modify, delete}, {}, {}], sign}, {}]

Fig. 23. Decomposition of the non atomic business activity "absorption by qualification"

In this decomposition, the abstract business activity "absorption by qualification" is implemented by two optional business activities.

The refinement of a logical view (see Figure 24 for the formal definition) replaces the decomposed business activity by its decomposition and integrates the new variability constraints in the new model.

Input: - A logical perspective *lp* of an organization, - A decomposition *D* of a non atomic business activity *a* of *lp*.
Output: A specific logical view perspective *LMR(lp, D)* of an application domain
Construction schema: *LMR (lp,D)= (LMR .name(lp,D), LMR.descriptor(lp,D), LMR .realization(lp,D))*
Semantics rules: 1. *LMR .name(lp,D) = name(lp)* 2. *LMR.descriptor(lp,D) = descriptor(lp)* 3. *LMR .realization(lp,D) = (LMR .solution(lp,D), LMR . adaptation _points (lp,D))* 3.1. *LMR .solution(lp,D) = solution(realization(lp))* 3.2. *LMR. Adaptation_ points (lp,D) = adaptationpoints (realization(lp))* **if** $(optional(D) = \varnothing \wedge variabilities(D) = \varnothing)$ **and** *LMR . adaptation _points (lp,D) = adaptationpoints (realization(lp))* $\cup$ *{(m, variants(m))}* **if** $optional(D) \neq \varnothing \vee variabilities(D) \neq \varnothing$

Fig. 24. The logical view refinement rule

Figure 26 shows the result of the refinement of the logical view of the civil servant management information system (Figure 25) based on the decomposition of Figure 23.

Name: *Logical model of the recruitment of personals governed by the general status or the labor code in the Cameroonian civil servant management information system.*

Descriptor *:*

Intention *: (specify)* $_{ACTION}$ *((recruit = [{}, { absorb by qualification, absorb by competitive examination, contractualize, engage}, {}}])*$_{ACTION}$*(candidates, applications, competitive examination, civil servants governed by the general status or the labor code, decisions)*$_{TARGET}$*(If the candidate has succeeded a competitive examination or has obtained a diploma giving the right to absorption or the Presidency of the Republic has given the authorization)*$_{DETAIL}$ *)*$_{TARGET}$

Context *:*

Domain : C = (manage)$_{ACTION}$*(career, salaries, training, network, mail, system)*$_{TARGET}$

Process: C_{111} *= (recruit = [{}, {absorb by qualification, absorb by competitive examination, contractualize, engage}, {}}])*$_{ACTION}$*(candidates, applications, competitive examinations, civil servants governed by the general status or the labor code, decisions)*$_{TARGET}$*(If the candidate has succeeded a competitive examination or has obtained a diploma giving the right to absorption or the Presidency of the Republic has given the authorization)*$_{DETAIL}$

/ sub process of the process* C_{111} **/*

(absorb by qualification)$_{ACTION}$ *({decision, civil servants governed by the general status})* $_{TARGET}$

(absorb by competitive examination)$_{ACTION}$ *({decision, civil servant governed by the general status})* $_{TARGET}$

(contractualize)$_{ACTION}$ *({decision, civil servant governed by the labor code})* $_{TARGET}$

(engage)$_{ACTION}$ *({decision, civil servant governed by the labor code })* $_{TARGET}$

Realization *:*

Solution *:*

pseudonym : recruit;

parameters: {candidates, applications, competitive examination, civil servants, decisions};

task: < {}, {absorb by qualification, absorb by competitive examination, contractualize, engage}, {}>;

include: ***FModule****;*

external: ***FModule****]*

specification: ***PseudoCode***

Adaptation points *:*

{}

Fig. 25. A logical view of Cameroon civil servant management IS

```
                              . . .
Realization :
  Solution :
      pseudonym : recruit;
      parameters: {candidates, applications, competitive examinations, civil servants, decisions};
  task: < {}, {absorb by qualification = [{}, {prepare = [{initiate, validate, append visa, remove
      validation, modify, delete}, {}, {}], sign}, {}], absorb by competitive examination,
      contractualize, engage}, {}>;
      include: FModule;
      external: FModule]
      specification: PseudoCode
  Adaptation points :
                    {(absorb by qualification,
                         {{prepare},
                         {sign},
                         {prepare, sign}})
                                              }
```

Fig. 26. A refined logical view of Cameroon civil servant management IS

4. Conclusion

Until the last decade, variability could be defined either as an integral part of development artefacts or in a separate variability model. Concerning the first trend, many research contributions have suggested the integration of variability in traditional software development diagrams or models such as use case models (Oliviera et al., 2005), feature models (Kang et al., 2002; Bashroush et al., 2008), message sequence diagrams (Ziadi, 2004), class diagrams (Clauss, 2001; Ziadi, 2004), and activity diagrams (Razavian et al., 2008) to represent variability. Many others approaches have been proposed that suggest to define the variability information in a separate "orthogonal variability model" (OVM) which, according to Pohl et al. (2005), is a model that explicitly defines the variability of a software product line. In this chapter, we have presented an approach that tries to reconcile the two precedent orientations. The main idea is to envelop assets of a domain-specific design method managing variability with a domain knowledge layer which provides for each asset the context in which it can be reused. The domain knowledge layer is in fact an OVM that highlights the variability of the assets.

The resulting SPL engineering methodology has domain engineering activities, referred to as the horizontal engineering process, whose aim is to develop a product lines's reusable core assets to provide a production capability for products, and application engineering activities, referred to as the vertical engineering process, whose aim is to generate new systems utilizing the assets developed by horizontal engineering; The ultimate goal of the vertical engineering process is therefore to configure a suitable business application from domain engineering.

5. References

Atsa, E.R., Fouda, N.M., Priso, E.N. & Abessolo, A.G. (2010). Improving the quality of service of a public service workflow based on ant theory: A case study in Cameroon. *The Electronic Journal of Information Systems in Developing Countries*, Vol.41(1),pp. 1-15.

Bashroush, R., Spence, I., Kilpatrick, P., Brown, T.J., Gillan, C. (2008). Multiple Views Models for Variability Management in Software Product Lines. *Second International Workshop on Variability Modeling of Software Intensive System (VaMoS'08)*, Essen, Germany.

Bernus, P. (2003). Enterprise Models For Enterprise Architecture and ISO9000:2000. *Annual Reviews in Control*, 27, pp. 211-220.

Clauss, M. (2001). Generic Modelling Using UML Extensions for Variability. *Workshop on Domain Specific Visual Languages*, pp 11-18.

Eriksson, M., Börstler, J. & Borg, K. (2010). A Systems Product Line Approach, In: *Applied Software Product Line Engineering*, Kyo C. Kang, Vijayan Sugumaran, Sooyong Park, pp. 109-139, Crc Press, Taylor & Francis Group, ISBN 978-1-4200-6841-2, Boca Raton.

Fouda, N.M. & Amougou, N. (2009). The Feature Oriented Reuse Method with Business Component Semantics. *International Journal of Computer Science and Applications*, Vol. 6, No. 4, pp 63-83.

Fouda, N.M. & Amougou, N. (2010). Product Lines' Feature-Oriented Engineering for Reuse: A Formal Approach. *International Journal of Computer Science Issues*, Vol. 7, Issue 5, pp 382-393.

Fox, M.S. & Gruninger, M. (1998). Enterprise Modeling, *AI Magazine Fall 1998*, pp. 109-121.

Kang, K.C., Lee, K., Lee, J. & Kim, S. (2003). Feature-Oriented Product Line Software Engineering: Principles and Guidelines. *Domain Oriented Systems Development: Perspectives and Practices*, K. Itoh et al., eds., pp. 29-46.

Kang, K.C., Sugumaran, V. & Park, S. (2010). Software Product Line Engineering: Overview and Future Direction, In: *Applied Software Product Line Engineering*, Kyo C. Kang, Vijayan Sugumaran, Sooyong Park, pp. 3-14, Crc Press, Taylor & Francis Group, ISBN 978-1-4200-6841-2, Boca Raton.

Kang, K.C., Kim, S., Shin, E. & Huh, M. (1998). "FORM: A Feature-Oriented Reuse Method with Domain-Specific Reference Architectures", *Annals of Software Engineering*, Vol. 5, pp. 143-168.

Kang, K.C., Lee, J. & Donohoe, P. (2002). Feature-Oriented Product Line Engineering. *IEEE Software*, Vol. 19, no. 4, pp. 58-65.

Lankhorst, M. (2004). Enterprise Architecture Modeling - The Issue of Integration. *Advanced Engineering Informatics*, 18, pp 205-216.

Lee, K., Kang, K.C. & Choi, W. (2000). Feature-Based Approach to Object-Oriented Engineering of Applications for Reuse. *Software-Practice and Experience*, 30, pp.1025-1046.

Northrop, L. (2002). SEI's software product line tenets. *IEEE Software* 19 (4): 32–40.

Oliviera, E.A., Gimenes, I., Huzita, E., Maldonado, J.C. (2005). Variability Management Process for Software Product Lines. *In Proc. of CASCON 2005*, Toronto, Canada.

Partsch, H.A. (1990). Specification and transformation of programs: A Formal Approach To Software Development. *Springer-Verlag New York, Inc.* New York, USA.

Pohl, K., Bockle, G., Linden, F.V.D., (2005). Software Product Line Engineering: Foundations, Principles, and Techniques. *Springer-Verlag Berlin,* Heidelberg.

Ramadour, P. & Cauvet, C. (2002). Approach and Model for Business Components Specification, *Proceeding of the 13th International Conference on Database and Expert Systems Applications, Lecture Notes In Computer Science*; Vol. 2453, pp 628-637.

Ramadour, P. (2001). Modèles et langage pour la conception et la manipulation de composants réutilisables de domaine. *PhD thesis*, Université d'Aix-Marseille III, Marseille, France.

Razavian, M., Khosravi, R. (2008). Modeling Variability in Business Process Models Using UML. *Fifth International Conference on Information Technology: New Generations*, Las Vegas, USA.

Recker, J., Mendling, J., van der Aalst, W. & Rosemann, M. (2006). Model-driven Enterprise Systems Configuration, *Proceeding of the 18th International Conference of Advanced Information Systems Engineering, CAiSE 2006*, Luxembourg, Lectures Notes in Computer Science, Vol. 4001, pp. 369-383, Springer.

Rosemanna, M. & van der Aalst, W.M.P. (2003). A Configurable Reference Modelling Language. *QUT Technical Report, FIT-TR-2003-05*, Queensland University of Technology, Brisbane, Australia.

Rotenstreich, S. (1992). Transformational Approach to Software Design. *Information Software Technology*, Volume 34, Issue 2, pp 106-116.

Subramanian, N. & Chung, L. (2001a). Software Architecture Adaptability: An NFR Approach, *Proceeding of the 4th International Workshop on Principles of Software Evolution*, New-York, USA, ACM Digital Library.

Subramanian, N. & Chung, L. (2001b). Metrics for Software Adaptability, *Software Quality Management Conference.*

van der Linden, F., Schmid, K. & Rommes, E. (2007). *Software product lines in action: The best industrial practice in product line engineering*, Berlin: Springer-Verlag.

Vernadat, F.P. (2002). Enterprise Modeling and Integration (EMI): Current Status and Research Perspectives. *Annual Reviews in Control*, 26, pp. 15-25.

Weiss, D.M. & Lai, C.T.R. (1999). *Software product line engineering: A family-based software development process*, Boston: Addison-Wesley Longman.

Whitten, J.L., Bentley, L.D. & Dittman, K.C. (2001). *Systems Analysis and Design Methods*, 5th ed., McGraw-Hill Companies, Inc.

Zachman, J. (1987). A Framework for Information System Architecture. *IBM Systems Journal*, Vol. 26(3).

Ziadi, T. (2004). Manipulation de Lignes de Produits en UML. *Phd Thesis,* Université de Rennes I, France.

Part 2

Analysis

4

Integrating Performance Analysis in Software Product Line Development Process

Rasha Tawhid and Dorina Petriu
Carleton University
Canada

1. Introduction

A Software Product Line (SPL) is a set of similar software systems that share a common set of features satisfying a particular domain, and are built from a shared set of software assets using a common means of production. Experience shows that by adopting a SPL development approach, organizations achieved increased quality and significant reductions in cost and time to market [Clements & Northrop, 2001].

Model-Driven Development (MDD) is a well-known paradigm that aims at capturing every important aspect of software development through models. An emerging trend apparent in the recent literature is that the SPL development moves toward adopting a MDD paradigm, which means that models are increasingly used to represent software artifacts of the family or of individual products [Groher & Voelter, 2009]. MDD plays an important role in the verification of non-functional properties (such as performance, reliability, security) of UML software models extended with information specific to the property to be evaluated [Woodside et al., 2005]. UML software models can be annotated with performance properties by using the *UML Performance Profile for Modeling and Analysis of Real-Time and Embedded Systems (MARTE)* [OMG, 2011] recently standardized by OMG.

This chapter presents a comprehensive methodology for integrating performance analysis in the early phases of SPL model-driven development process, whose goal is to evaluate the performance characteristic of different products by generating and analyzing quantitative performance models [Tawhid & Petriu, 2008a, 2008b]. We start by adding generic performance annotations expressed in MARTE to the UML model representing the set of core reusable SPL assets. A model transformation realized in the Atlas Transformation Language (ATL) derives the UML model of a specific product with concrete MARTE performance annotations from the SPL model. The product derivation process binds the variability expressed in the SPL to a specific product, and also the generic SPL performance annotations to concrete values provided by the designer for this product. The proposed model transformation approach can be applied to any existing SPL model-driven development process using UML for modeling software.

It is known that one of the main concepts of software product line development is to take advantage of the reusability of the set of core assets shared among the members of a family of products, instead of building each product from scratch. In this work, we apply the same reusability concept to the performance annotations, by integrating software performance engineering techniques in the early phases of SPL development. Instead of annotating from scratch each UML model of each product, we propose to annotate the SPL model once with generic annotations, and to provide binding information when deriving the annotated model of a desired product from the generic SPL model.

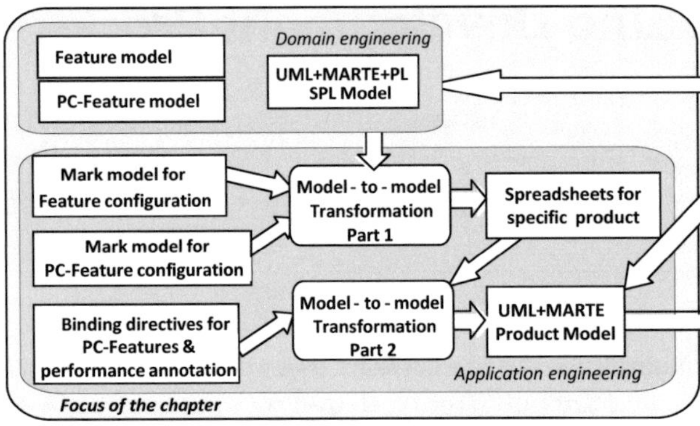

Fig. 1. Approach for deriving a product performance model

The objective of the research presented in this chapter is to automatically generate a performance model for a given product from a performance-annotated SPL model. The main research challenge originates from the mismatch between the meanings of the two models. While a SPL model is a set of core "generic" asset models that are building blocks for many different products with all kind of options and alternatives, a performance model is an instance-based representation of a runtime system, focusing on how the system is using available resources and how competition for resources impacts the system performance (response time, throughput, utilization, etc.) The derivation of a performance model requires two model transformations, as shown in Fig.1: a) from the annotated SPL model to a product model with performance annotations, and b) from the outcome of the first step to a performance model. The work presented here focuses on the first transformation as illustrated by the shaded area in Fig.1, whereas the second transformation for deriving automatically a Layered Queueing Network (LQN) performance model for a specific product applies the PUMA transformation approach previously developed in our research group [Woodside et al., 2005].

The automatic derivation of a specific product model based on a given feature configuration is enabled through the mapping between features from the feature model and their realizations in the design model. In this chapter, an efficient mapping technique is used, which aims to minimize the amount of explicit feature annotations in the UML design model of SPL. Implicit feature mapping is inferred during product derivation from the relationships between annotated and non-annotated model elements as defined in the UML metamodel [Tawhid & Petriu, 2011a].

Performance is a runtime property of the deployed system and depends on two types of factors: some are contained in the design model of the product (obtained from the SPL model) while others characterize the underlying platforms and runtime environment. Performance models need to reflect both types of factors. Woodside et al. proposed the concept of performance completions to close the gap between abstract design models and external factors [Woodside et al., 2002]. Performance completions provide a means to extend the modeling constructs of a system by including the influence of the underlying platforms and execution environments in performance evaluation models. Since our goal is to automate the derivation of a performance model for a specific product from the SPL model, we propose to deal with performance completions in the early phases of the SPL development process by introducing a so-called Performance Completion feature (PC-feature) model, which characterizes the variability in platform choices, execution environments, different types of communication realizations, and other external factors that have an impact on performance, such as different protocols for secure communication channels [Tawhid & Petriu, 2011b]. Performance model helps software developers explore various design alternatives. It also addresses the problem of domain evolution arising when an existing product runs on a new platform. In this chapter, we explain how this evolution can be propagated to the performance model through the PC-feature model.

The chapter is organized as follows: section 2 discusses related work; section 3 presents the domain engineering process where the SPL model and two different kinds of feature models are created; the model transformation approach for generating a given product model is illustrated with a case study in section 3; section 4 analyzes the performance effects of different security levels for communication channels running on two different architectures; and section 5 presents the conclusions.

2. Related work

This section presents related research on product derivation approaches and different feature mapping techniques. Work related to performance analysis of software system, addressing quality attributes in SPL is also discussed.

Voelter et al. propose an approach that integrates aspect-oriented (AOSD) and model-driven software development (MDSD) techniques to support variability management and product derivation [Groher & Voelter, 2009]. Two different ways of dealing with variability are identified: a) negative variability which selectively removes parts of a model based on the presence or absence of features in the configuration model; b) positive variability which starts with a minimal core of common SPL artifacts and selectively adds additional product-specific parts through model weaving. Our approach applies a similar concept of positive variability through automatic model transformation. In [Stoiber & Glinz, 2009], aspect-orientation is combined with table-based modeling by using the ADORA modeling language. An approach for deriving the architecture of a product by selectively copying elements from the SPL architecture (which covers all possible product aspects) based on a product-specific feature configuration is proposed in [Botterweck et al., 2009]. This approach is concerned only with the derivation of the high-level product architecture, while our approach derives both the structural and behavioural views of the product design model. An Eclipse-based tool called FeatureMapper that defines the mapping of features in the problem space to model elements realizing these features in the solution space is proposed in [Heidenreich et al., 2007, 2008]. The set of selected features for a product combined with the mapping model are interpreted by the FeatureMapper transformation component to derive a product model.

An approach for expressing variability in a family model based on a *feature-based model template* by mapping features to model elements realizing them is introduced in [Czarnecki et al., 2005a, 2005b]. Each model element is annotated with a presence condition (PC), indicating whether the element should be present in a template instance or not. The model template is automatically instantiated by evaluating the PCs for a given feature configuration. The concept of negative variability is applied, by removing model elements whose PC evaluates to false. A drawback of this approach is that the model template is cluttered with variability specifications for each model element. Some issues related to the behavioural derivation of a given product model are discussed in [Istoan et al., 2011]. It is shown that the composition order is significant when using Aspect-Oriented modeling, since different orders for composing sequence diagrams leads to different derived products.

A model-driven approach for SPL evolution is proposed in [Gamez & Fuentes, 2011], which automatically propagates the evolution changes of a cardinality-based FM into existing configurations.

The Product Line UML-Based Software Engineering (PLUS) method introduced in [Gomaa, 2005] provides several concepts and stereotypes to express variability in multiple views of SPL. The mapping between features and the model elements realizing them is introduced through a separate tabular representation of feature/use case and feature/class relationships. Our approach introduces a different mapping technique by annotating each class and use case with the feature(s) requiring it. The automatic derivation of a concrete product from the SPL model according to a set of chosen features is not addressed in [Gomaa, 2005]. The PLUS method is extended in [Street & Gomaa, 2006] to specify performance requirements by introducing several stereotypes specific to model performance requirements such as «optional» and «alternative performance feature». Although feature modeling is essential in SPL, the concept of "feature" is not a first-class model element in UML. In order to overcome this problem, different stereotypes for representing features and feature dependency have been defined in literature (however, none is standard yet). Our variability profile is based on Gomaa's work, especially on PLUS [Gomaa, 2005]. However, our approach has the following main differences from PLUS: a) we proposed an automatic derivation of a product model from a SPL model; b) we deal with MARTE performance annotations, both in the source and target models; c) we use sequence diagrams for behaviour representation taking advantage of their enhanced modeling power,; d) we introduce variability within a sequence diagram through *Combined Fragments;* e) we introduce the so-called *Performance Completion feature model.*

Several works have been done on performance analysis addressing quality attributes in SPL. A method for designing parametric performance completions that are independent of a specific platform is proposed in [Happe et al., 2010]. The completions can be instantiated for different environments by explicitly coupling the transformations to performance models and implementation to add the necessary details to both.

Model-driven development and SPL paradigms are integrated together to model embedded software systems in [Belategi et al., 2010a]. An analysis method taking into account scenarios, platform, and variability for embedded SPL has been proposed. Although the authors consider the SPL architecture as a critical asset for representing quality attributes and their compliance to quality goals, they have not addressed how quality attributes are modeled in the architecture. In [Belategi et al., 2010b], the MARTE profile is analyzed to identify the variability mechanisms of the profile in order to model variability in embedded SPL models. Although MARTE was not defined for product lines, the paper proposes to combine it with existing mechanisms for representing variability, but it does not explain how this can be achieved. A model analysis process for embedded SPL is presented in [Belategi et al., 2011] to validate and verify quality attributes variability. The concept of multilevel and staged feature model is applied by introducing more than one feature models that represent different information at different abstraction levels; however, the traceability links between the multilevel models and the design model are not explained. In [Bartholdt et al., 2009] the authors propose an integrated tool-supported approach that considers both qualitative and quantitative quality attributes without imposing hierarchical structural constraints. The integration of SPL quality attributes is addressed by assigning quality attributes to software elements in the solution domain and linking these elements to features. An aggregation function is used to collect the quality attributes depending on the selected features for a given product. An approach called Svamp is proposed to model functional and quality variability at the architectural level of the SPL [Raatikainen et al., 2008]. The approach integrates several models: a Kumbang model to represent the functional and structural variability in the architecture and to define components that are used by other models; a quality attribute model to specify the quality properties and a quality variability model for expressing variability within these quality attributes. The Model-Driven Architecture approach is extended in [Cortellessa et al., 2007] with non-functional modeling and analysis concepts by adding new models and transformations for validation activities. The concepts of platform independent and platform specific are used through the new type of models to obtain an accurate validation.

To the best of our knowledge, in the context of SPL, no work has been done previously to evaluate and predict the performance of a given product by generating a formal performance model. Most of the existing work aims to model non-functional requirements (NFRs) in the same way as functional requirements. The related works mentioned above are concerned with the interactions between selected features and the NFRs and propose different techniques to represent these interactions and dependencies.

3. Domain engineering process

The SPL development process is separated into two major phases: 1) *domain engineering* for creating and maintaining a set of reusable artifacts and introducing variability in these software artifacts so that the next phase can make a specific decision according to the product's requirements and 2) *application engineering* for building products that are family members from reusable artifacts created in the first phase, instead of starting from scratch.

The domain engineering process is a development cycle *for* reuse and includes, but is not limited to, creating the requirement specifications, domain models , architecture, reusable software components [Clements & Northrop, 2001].

The SPL assets created by the domain engineering process which are of interest for our research are represented by a multi-view UML design model of the family, called the *SPL model*, consisting of a superimposition of all variant products. The creation of the SPL model employs two separate UML profiles: a *product line* profile for specifying the commonality and variability between products, and the MARTE profile for performance annotations. Another important outcome of the domain engineering process is the feature model used to represent commonalities and variabilities between family members in a concise taxonomic form. Additionally, the PC-feature model is created to represent the variability space of the performance completions.

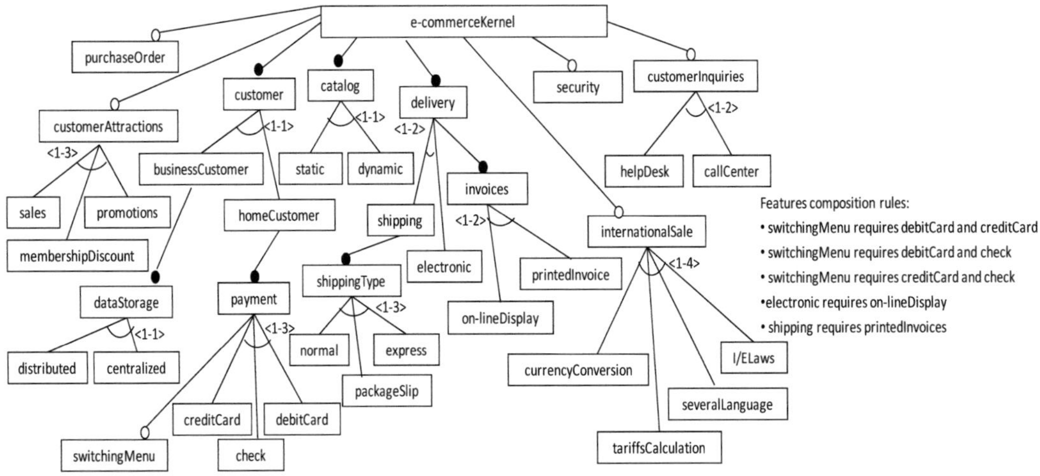

Fig. 2. Feature model of the e-commerce SPL

An e-commerce case study is used to illustrate the construction of the UML model for SPL that represents the source model of our model transformation approach. The e-commerce SPL is a web-based product line that can generate a distributed application that can handle either business-to-business (B2B) or business-to-consumer (B2C) systems. For instance, in B2B, a business customer can browse and select items through several catalogs. Each customer has a contract with a supplier for purchases, as well as bank accounts through which payments can be made. An operation fund is associated with each contract.

3.1 Feature model

Feature models are used in our approach to represent two different variability spaces. This section describes the regular feature model representing functional variabilities between products. The feature model of an e-commerce SPL is represented in Fig. 2 in the extended FODA notation, Cardinality-Based Feature Model (CBFM) [Czarnecki et al., 2005]. However, this diagram is represented in the source model given as input to our ATL transformation as an extended UML class diagram, where the features and feature groups are modeled as stereotyped classes and the dependencies and constraints between features as stereotyped associations. For instance, the two alternative features *BusinessCustomer* and *HomeCustomer* are mutually exclusive features and hence they are grouped into an *exactly-one-of* feature group called *Customer*. While, the three optional features *CreditCard, DebitCard,* and *Check* are grouped into an *at-least-one-of* feature group called *Payment*. Thus, an individual system can provide at least one of these features or any number of them. In the case of an individual system providing all of these features, the user can choose one of them during the run-time execution. In addition to functional features, we add to the diagram another type of features characterizing design decisions that have an impact on the non-functional requirements or properties. For example, the architectural decision related to the location of the data storage (centralized or distributed) affects performance, reliability and security, and is represented in the diagram by two mutually exclusive quality features. This type of feature related to a SPL design decision is part of the design model, not just a platform-related PC-feature required only for performance analysis.

The regular feature model represents the set of all possible combinations of features for the products of the family, describing the way features can be combined within this SPL. A specific product is configured by selecting a valid feature combination from the feature model, producing the feature configuration based on the product's requirements. To enable the automatic derivation of a given product model, the mapping between the features contained in the feature model and their realizations in a reusable SPL model needs to be specified, as shown in the next section. Also, each stereotyped class in the feature model has a tagged value indicating whether it is selected in a given feature configuration or not.

3.2 SPL model

The SPL model should contain, among other assets, structural and behavioural views which are essential for the derivation of performance models. It consists of: 1) structural description of the software showing the high-level classes or components, especially if they are distributed and/or concurrent; 2) deployment of software to hardware devices; 3) a set of key performance scenarios defining the main system functions frequently executed.

The functional requirements of the SPL are modeled as use cases shown in Fig. 3. The kernel use cases required by all the family members are shown in white, the optional use cases that may be used by any member are drawn in light grey, and the alternative use cases used only by some members are shown in dark grey. In order to avoid polluting our model with extra annotations and to ensure the well-formedness of the derived product model, we propose to annotate explicitly the minimum number of model elements within each diagram of our SPL model. For instance, in the use case diagram, only the optional and alternative use cases are annotated with the name of the features requiring them (given as stereotype attributes); since a kernel use case represents commonality, it is sufficient to just stereotype it as «kernel». Other model elements, such as actors, associations, generalizations, properties, are mapped implicitly to feature through their relationship with the use cases, so there is no need to clutter the model with their annotations. The evaluation of implicit mapping during product derivation is explained in section 4. The structural view of the SPL is presented as a class diagram; Fig. 4 depicts a small fragment. The classes that are common to all members of the SPL are stereotyped as «kernel». The variability that distinguishes the members of a family from each other is explicitly modeled by classes stereotyped as «optional» or «variant»; such classes are also annotated with the name of the feature(s) requiring them (given as stereotype attributes). This is an example of mapping between features and the model elements realizing them.

In cases where a class behaves differently in different product (such as *CustomerInterface* in B2B and B2C systems) a generalization/specialization hierarchy is used to model the different behaviours of this class. The two subclasses *B2BInterface* and *B2CInterface* are used by B2B systems and B2C systems, respectively. The same happens with the superclass *SupplierInterface*, which is specialized into two variants *POSupplier* and *Supplier*.

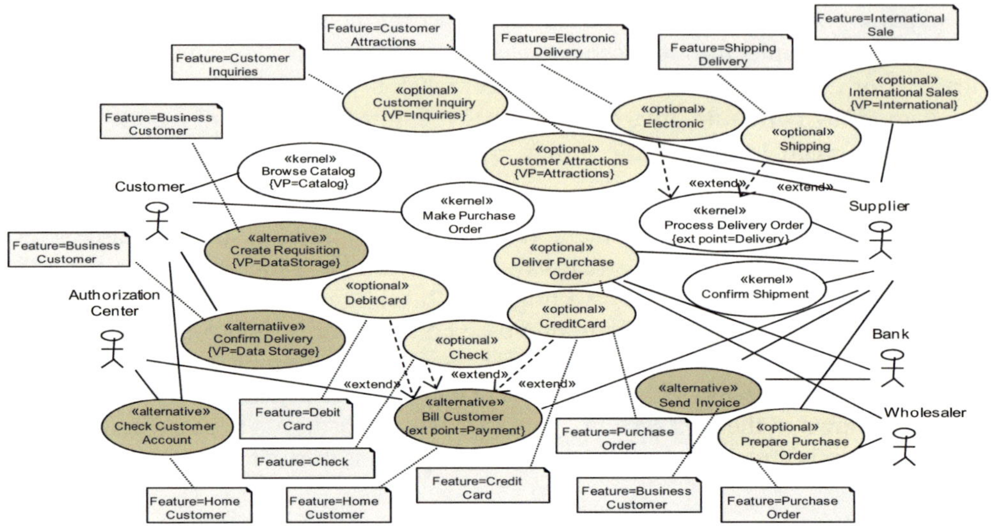

Fig. 3. Use case model of the e-commerce SPL

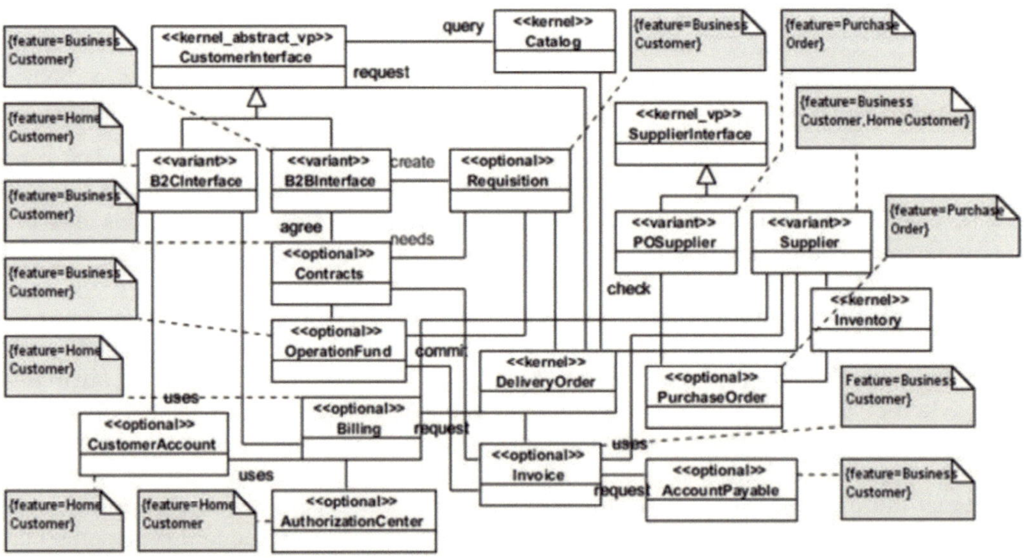

Fig. 4. A fragment of the class diagram of the e-commerce SPL

The behavioural SPL view is modeled as sequence diagrams for each scenario of each use case. Fig. 5 illustrates the alternative scenario *Create Requisition*. Variability in the sequence diagram may be expressed by using *alt* or *opt* fragments stereotyped as «variation point». For example, the *alt* fragment stereotyped with «variation point» {vp=*Data Storage*} gives two alternative choices based on the value of the Data Storage feature (Distributed or Centralized). The stereotypes in Fig. 5 are MARTE performance annotations [OMG, 2011]. «GaAnalysisContext» is a stereotype indicating that the entire interaction diagram is to be considered for performance analysis. Each lifeline is stereotyped as «PaRunTInstance», providing an explicit connection at the annotation level between a role in a behavior definition (a lifeline) and a runtime instance of a process or thread (active object). For example, the tag {instance= CBrowser} indicates which runtime instance of a process executes the lifeline role, while the tag {host=$CustNode} indicates the physical node from the deployment diagram on which the instance is running, given by the variable $CustNode. (For convenience, we use names starting with '$' for all MARTE variables). Conceptually, a scenario represented by a UML sequence diagram is composed of units of execution named steps. MARTE defines two kinds of steps for performance analysis: execution step (stereotyped «PaStep») and communication step (stereotyped «PaCommStep»). «PaStep» may be applied to an Execution Occurrence (represented as a thin rectangle on the lifeline) or to the message that triggers it. For instance, in Fig. 5, the message *requisitionRequest* is stereotyped as an execution step:

«PaStep» {hostDemand = ($ReqSD,ms), respT = (($ReqT,ms, percent95), calc)}

where hostDemand indicates the execution time required by the step, given by the variable $ReqSD in time units of milliseconds. The same message *requisitionRequest* is also stereotyped as a communication step:

«PaCommStep» { msgSize = ($MReq,KB)}

where the message size is the variable $MReq in KiloBytes. Note that since the SPL model is generic, covering many products and containing variation points with variants, the MARTE annotations need to be generic as well. We use MARTE variables as a means of parameterizing the SPL performance annotations; such variables (parameters) will be assigned (bound to) concrete values during the product derivation process. The workload of a scenario is defined as a stream of events driving the system; a workload may be open or closed. In our example the workload is closed with a number of users $N1 and user think time for a user $Z1:

«GaWorkloadEvent» {pattern=(closed (population=$N1),(extDelay=$Z1))}

3.3 Performance completions

In SPL, different members may vary from each other in terms of their functional requirements, quality attributes, platform choices, network connections, physical configurations, and middleware. Many details contained in the system that are not part of its design model, but still affecting the performance at run-time, need to be added to the performance model. Performance completions, as proposed by Woodside [Woodside et al., 2002], are a manner to add platform details, closing the gap between the high-level design model and its different implementations. Performance completions provide a general concept to include low-level details of execution environments in performance models.

Since performance analysis depends on the software to hardware allocation, another structure diagram that is not usually represented in SPL models has to be provided in our approach. The deployment diagram for the SPL is built assuming maximum distribution, which means providing the largest number of processors that might ever be used for any product of the SPL. However, it doesn't mean providing a processor for every single artifact manifesting an instance of an active or passive class. If it is known that some instances have to run always on the same processor, they will be co-allocated on the same node. The

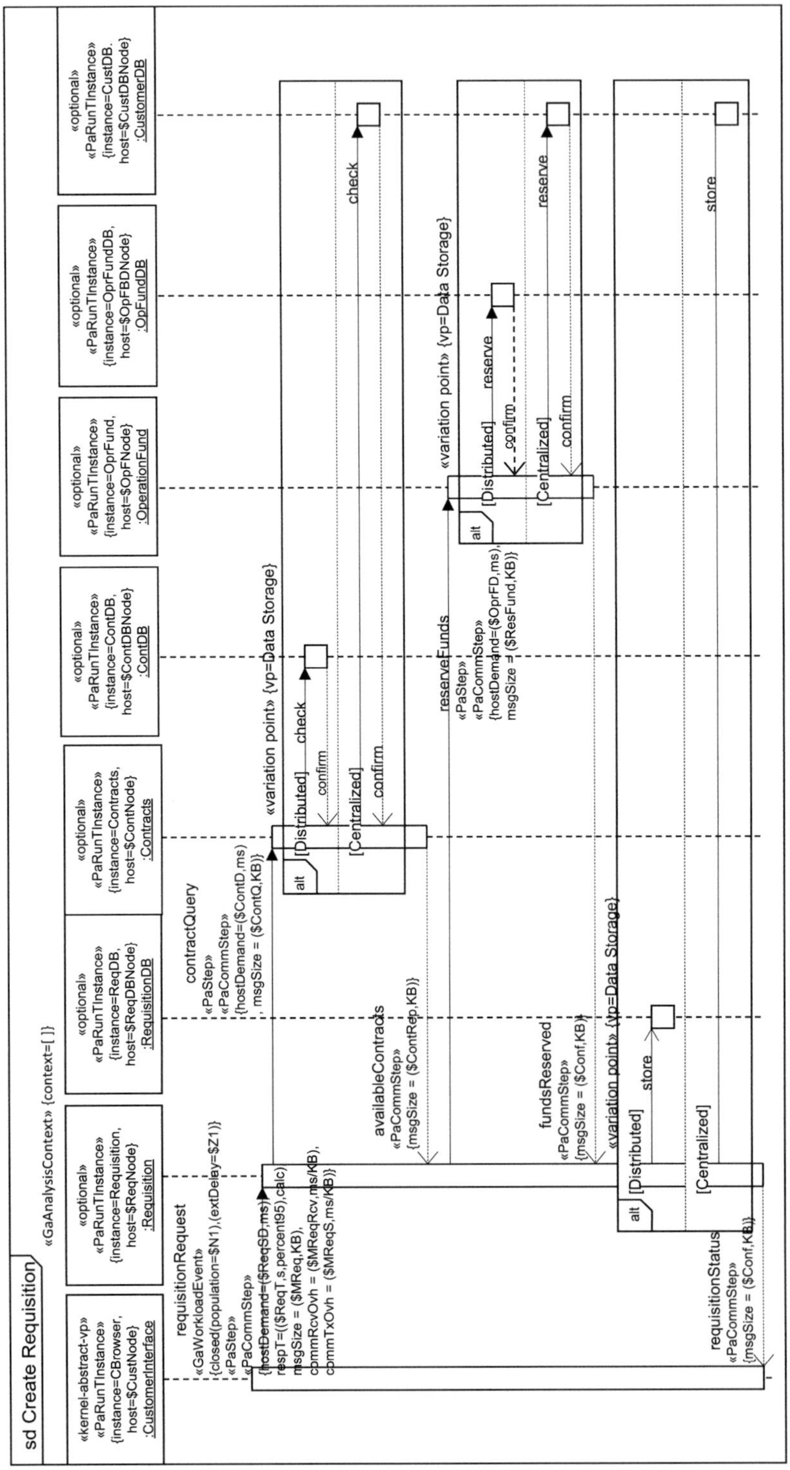

Fig. 5. SPL Scenario Create Requisition

deployment diagram contains all the possible artifacts contained in all the products, even artifacts corresponding to optional or variant classes. During the domain engineering process for our case study, two different deployment diagrams for the SPL system are provided, distributed and centralized, corresponding to the two alternative architectures.

This section covers the variability space of the performance completions and represents it through the Performance Completion feature model (PC-feature model) shown in Fig. 6. Each feature from the PC-feature model may affect one or more performance attributes. For instance, data compression reduces the message size and at the same time increases the processor communication overhead for compressing and decompressing the data. Thus, it is mapped to the performance attributes message size and communication overhead through the MARTE attributes *msgSize*, *commTxOvh* and *commRcvOvh*, respectively. The mapping here is between a PC-feature and the performance attribute(s) it affects, which are MARTE stereotype attributes associated to model elements. Table 1 illustrates this type of mapping between PC-features and the design model, set up through the MARTE stereotypes attached to model elements.

Adding security solutions requires more resources and longer execution times, which in turn has a significant impact on system performance. We introduce a PC-feature group called *secureCommunication* that contains two alternative features *secured* and *unsecured*. The *secured* feature offers two security protocols: Secure Socket Layer (SSL) and Transport Layer Security (TLS) that can be augmented to the applications. Furthermore, we introduce three security level alternatives depending on the size of the key used in the handshake phase and on the strength of the encryption and message digest algorithms used in the data transfer phase, as proposed in [Menasce et al., 2004]. Each security level requires different extra times for sending and receiving secure messages. These overheads are mapped to the communication overheads in the deployment diagram through the attributes *commRcvOvh* and *commTxOvh*, which represent the host demand overheads for receiving and sending messages, respectively.

Each type of communication channel has different capacity for the amount of information that can be transmitted over this channel. As the channel's capacity increases, the time for data transmitted over this channel decreases. Our example provides three different communication channels with three alternative connections for the Internet. The capacity and latency for each physical channel type are respectively mapped to the attributes *capacity* and *blockT* stereotyping each communication node in the deployment diagram.

PC-feature	Affected Performance Attribute	MARTE Stereotype	MARTE Attribute
secureCommunication	Communication overhead	GAExecHost	commRcvOvh commTxOvh
channelType	Channel Capacity Channel Latency	GaCommHost	capacity blockT
dataCompression	Message size Communication overhead	PaCommStep GAExecHost	msgSize commRcvOvh commTxOvh
externalDeviceType	Service Time	PaStep	extOpDemand
messageType	Communication overhead	GAExecHost	commTxOvh

Table 1. Mapping of PC-features to affected performance attributes

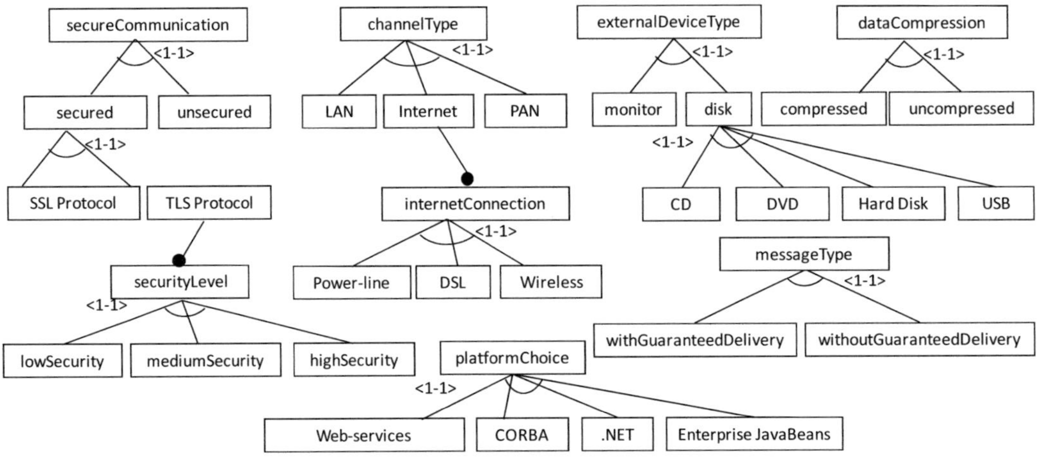

Fig. 6. Part of the Performance-Completion feature model of the e-commerce SPL

Data compression requires extra operations which increase the processing time, but at the same time compression helps reducing the use of resources, such as hard disk space or communication channel bandwidth. Data compression/decompression is adding an overhead when sending and receiving a message, which is mapped to the attributes *commTxOvh* and *commRcvOvh*, respectively. However, compression reduces the amount of data to be transferred and decreases the delivery time (e.g., a compression algorithm may reduce the size of data to 60% [Happe et al., 2010]). Thus, the amount of compressed data transmitted over a physical channel is mapped to the performance attribute message size through the attribute *msgSize* of a stereotype «PaCommStep» annotating a communication step in the sequence diagram. Similarly, the delivery time of a message may vary if the communication is with or without guaranteed delivery [Happe et al., 2010], which affects the attribute *commTxOvh*.

Mapping a platform independent to a platform specific model has an impact on the system performance. The PC-feature group *platformChoice* includes different alternative types of middleware such as CORBA, Web-services, etc., which will affect also the communication overheads.

MARTE provides specifically the concept of "external service calls" to represent resources that are not explicitly modeled within the UML design model, but may have an impact on performance. Examples of such external calls are disk operations hidden in database calls. The feature *externalDeviceType* represents different choices of storage devices, such as disk and monitor and different disk types. Each device has different speed to "read" and "write" a block of data. These features are mapped to the service time of external resources through the attribute *externalOpCount* stereotyping an execution step.

It is important to note that some of the performance-affecting attributes are contained directly in the MARTE annotations in the design model. For instance, the message size corresponding to a message from a sequence diagram may be indicated by the attribute *msgSize* of the stereotype «PaCommStep» extending the message. Similarly, CPU execution times of different scenario steps are indicated by the attribute *hostDemand* of the stereotype «PaStep». The product model obtained by the transformation presented next will include both the performance attribute contained directly in the design model and the platform factors corresponding to PC-features.

4. Model transformation approach

The automatic derivation of a concrete product model based on a given feature configuration is enabled through the mapping between features from the feature model and their realizations in the design model of the SPL. In this section, we present an efficient mapping technique that aims to minimize the amount of explicit feature annotations in the UML design model of SPL. The product model corresponding to the desired feature configuration is instantiated automatically through a model-to-model transformation, where the transformation process evaluates the SPL model elements' annotations for the selected feature configuration. The model transformation process and its implementation in ATL are presented as well.

4.1 Mapping technique

Modeling variability in SPL models can be achieved in different ways: 1) annotating different diagrams of the reusable SPL model with variability specifications mapping features from the feature model to model elements realizing them; and 2) using a separate model for variability that can be linked to different model elements of the reusable SPL model. In our work, we apply the first approach by using a product line (PL) profile similar to [Gomaa, 2005]. We are aiming to annotate the UML model of SPL with a minimum amount of variability specifications.

The annotation approach has a number of advantages over the separate variability modeling: a) model elements subject to variability are clearly noticeable; b) the consequence of selecting a feature is directly shown on the design model; c) the mapping is easier to retrace and understand; and d) the expressive capability is enhanced. However, a significant drawback of the annotation approach that makes it error-prone is the fact that the SPL models become cluttered with variability specifications, which becomes worse as models grow in size and complexity.

The annotation approach proposed in this research mitigates this drawback by reducing the type and number of explicitly annotated model elements as much as possible. The decision what types of elements to annotate explicitly depends on the application domain and should be taken early in the domain engineering process. The mapping of features to non-annotated model elements is implicit, and can be inferred from their relationships with annotated model elements. Such relationships are defined in the UML metamodel and are explored in the transformation rules during product derivation by navigating the model according to the UML metamodel and well-formedness rules. For instance, in a class diagram of the SPL reusable model, we annotate explicitly the variability of classes with the names of the features requiring each class, but leave the associations without variability annotations. The unspecified mapping of features to each association can be inferred from the annotations of the two classes connected to the association ends. Thus, the mapping of features to classes is explicit and that of features to associations is implicit. Whenever a model element is not explicitly annotated with corresponding feature(s) through a stereotype or its attributes in the SPL model, the automatic transformation process needs to decide whether to copy this element to the target model or not. This decision is based on several factors: a) the type of this non-annotated element; b) the specifications and well-formedness constraints of the modeling language; c) the presence or absence of other annotated elements related to it; d) the containment hierarchies defined in the metamodel; e) the cardinality of this element.

For example, according to the UML metamodel, a binary association has to be attached to a classifier at each end. Therefore, the decision whether a binary association has to be copied or not to the target is based on the selection of both of its classifiers. The binary association is created in the target model if and only if both of its *memberEnd* properties have their classifiers already selected and created. At the same time, if only one of its classifier is selected and created in the target model, the property attached to this unselected association and owned by the selected classifier should not be created in the target model. The interpretations of the implicit mapping will be explained in more detail in the description of the transformation rules.

The proposed mapping technique ensures that the derived product model is a well-formed model by enforcing the well-formedness constraints during the transformation process. Each time a new model element is selected and added to the target model, the verification of its well-formedness rules is guaranteed by construction, according to the transformation rules that are based on the UML metamodel.

4.2 Model transformation process

Our model transformation approach takes as input the SPL source model created during the domain engineering process in section 3 and generates a product target model for a given member of the SPL. The model transformation consists of two parts as shown in Fig. 1. The first part generates binding directive spreadsheets, asking the user to enter concrete values for all generic performance annotations and platform allocations for the given product, while the second part takes as input the spreadsheets with the concrete values provided by the user and generates a specific product model with concrete performance annotations that is deployed on concrete resources and is running on a specific platform. As mentioned before, our model transformation approach applies the concept of positive variability where we start by selecting and copying the SPL model elements that represent kernel features to the target model, then selectively add other elements realizing the desired optional and alternative features; all this is realized by a model transformation approach described below.

The product derivation process is initiated by specifying a given product through its feature configuration (i.e., the legal combination of features characterizing the product). The selected features are checked for consistency against the feature dependencies and constraints in the feature model, in order to identify any inconsistencies. An example is checking to ensure that no two mutually exclusive features are chosen. The feature configuration is considered a parameter for the transformation, which should be set without editing the source model. The second step in the derivation process is to select the use cases realizing the chosen features. All kernel use cases are copied to the product use case diagram, since they represent functionality provided by every member of the SPL. If a chosen feature is realized through extend or include relationships between use cases, both the base and the included or extending use cases have to be selected, as well. A use case containing in its scenario variation point(s) required to realize the selected feature(s) has to be chosen, too. The optional and alternative use cases are selected and copied to the target use case diagram if they are mapped to a feature from the feature configuration. The interpretations of other non-annotated elements will be explained in the description of the transformation rules. Finally, the use case diagram for the product is developed after all the PL variability stereotypes were eliminated. The third step is to derive the product class diagram by selecting first all kernel classes from the SPL class diagram. Optional and variant classes needed for the desired product are selected next (each is annotated with the feature(s) requiring it). Moreover, superclasses of the selected optional or variant classes have to be selected as well. The PL variability stereotypes are not copied to the target model. An association between two classes is copied to the target model if and only if both classes are selected.

The SPL deployment diagram has to be tailored to the concrete product in the fourth step. One of the two types of the deployment diagrams (centralized or distributed) has to be chosen based on the mutually exclusive feature group *DataStorage*. For instance, the centralized architecture is chosen and copied to the target model if the feature *centralized* is selected. The final step of the first part in our transformation approach is to generate the sequence diagrams corresponding to different scenarios of the chosen use cases. Each scenario of a chosen use case is recognized through a sequence diagram which has to be selected from the source model and copied to the target one.

The PL variability stereotypes are eliminated after binding the generic roles associated to the life-lines of each selected sequence diagram to specific roles corresponding to the chosen features. For instance, the sequence diagram *Create Requisition* has the generic alternate role *CustomerInterface* which has to be bound to the concrete role *B2BInterface* to realize the feature *BusinessCustomer*. However, the selection of the optional roles is based on the corresponding features. For instance, the generic optional role *CustomerDB* is selected if the feature *Centralized* data storage is chosen.

The mapping between the PC-features and performance attributes takes place during the first part of the model transformation and requires user input. The transformation extracts all the information needed for the mapping from the annotated product model and the PC-feature model, and generates spreadsheets for the given product. The second part of the model transformation takes as an input the spreadsheets with the values for bindings directives provided by the user, and produces the given product model with concrete values for performance annotations.

4.3 ATL implementation of the proposed approach

This subsection presents the implementation of the model transformation described in the previous subsection in the Atlas Transformation Language (ATL) [ATL], which is specialized for model transformations. The source model is the SPL model described in section 3 with two profiles applied, MARTE and PL, and the target model is that of a particular product. The transformation rules handle the implicit and explicit mapping of features to SPL design models. The ATL transformation is composed of a set of rules and helpers. The rules define the mapping between the source and target model, while the helpers are methods that can be called from different points in the ATL transformation. A few examples of ATL transformation rules are given bellow, with extensive comments in natural language.

We need to create in the target model all the model element types that compose a class diagram according to the UML metamodel: *Class, Property, Operation, Generalization, and Association* [OMG, 2007]. Since an optional or alternative class is annotated with the feature(s) requiring it, the class element is selected if and only if the feature given in its annotation is present in the feature configuration. The following rule is applied to each model element of type *Class* from the source model, checking whether to select and copy it to the target model. We need to distinguish between a property representing an attribute (related to the class by *ownedAttribute*) and a property representing an association end (related to an association by *memberEnd*). A property representing an attribute has to be selected if its container is selected. However, the one representing an association end is selected if and only if its class container and the related association are selected.

In order to select and copy to the target model only the associations between selected classes as well as their *memberEnds*, we have to navigate from the property of a selected class that represents an association end to the other end of the association and check whether the class on this end is selected or not. Assume that there are two classes: *ClassA* and *ClassB* connected with an association *AB*. *ClassA* owns a property *PA1* that has an attribute *type* referencing the other end of the association, *ClassB*. In turn, *PA1* has an attribute association referencing the association *AB*. The rule that interprets this implicit mapping navigates from the selected *ClassA* to the other end *ClassB* though the attribute *type* of the property *PA1* and checks whether *ClassB* is selected or not. If *ClassB* is selected, property *PA1* is selected as well. Last step is to navigate through the attribute *association* of property *PA1* to the association *AB*, and to copy it to the target model.

```
        -- Rule Class checks each model element of this type whether to copy it
        -- to the target model by calling the helper selectedElement()
rule Class {
        from
                s : UML! Class (s.selectedElement())
        -- Copying the class and checking for each property representing an
        -- association end whether the class on the other end of the association
        -- is selected or not
        to
                t : UML!Class(name <- s.name, ownedAttribute <-
                s.ownedAttribute->select(e | e.type.selectedElement())

        -- Whenever the class on the other end is selected, the property
        -- representing a memberEnd is copied to the target model by calling
        -- the lazy rule Property
                -> collect(e | thisModule.Property(e)),

        -- Copying the property owned by the class by calling the lazy rule
        -- Attribute
                ownedAttribute<-s.ownedAttribute->select(e | e.association
                ->oclIsUndefined())->collect(e | thisModule.Attribute(e)),

        -- Copying the operation owned by the class by calling the lazy rule
        -- Operation
```

```
            ownedOperation <- s.ownedOperation ->
             collect(e | thisModule.Operation(e)),
    -- Copying the generalization owned by the class by calling the lazy rule
     -- Generalization
                    generalization <- s.generalization
                    -> collect(e | thisModule.Generalization(e))) }
    -- This helper returns "true" if the respective element is selected by
    -- checking whether the tagged value of its stereotype's property
    -- existed in the feature configuration
    Helper context UML!Elementdef: selectedElement() : Boolean = if
    self.hasStereotype('kernel')
     or UML!Class.allInstances()->
     select(class | class.getTagValue('optionalfeature','selected')
     ='true'
     Or class.getTagValue('alternativefeature','selected')
     ='true')-> collect(c | c.name)->
     includes(self.getTagValue('variant','feature')
     or self.getTagValue('optional','feature') or
     self.getTagValue('alternative','feature'))
    then true else false
    endif;
    -- This helper returns "true" if the respective model element is
     -- stereotyped with the stereotype name given as a parameter
    Helper context UML!Elementdef: hasStereotype(stereotype:String)
     :Boolean = self.getAppliedStereotypes()->
     exists(c | c.name.startsWith(stereotype));
    -- This helper returns the tagged value of a stereotype's property both
     -- stereotype and property name are given as parameters
    Helper context UML!Elementdef:getTagvalue
    (stereotype:String,tag:String): UML!Element =
    if self.getAppliedStereotypes()-> select(e | e.name=stereotype)
    -> notEmpty() then
    self.getValue(self.getAppliedStereotypes() ->
    select(e | e.name=stereotype) -> first(), tag)
    else OclUndefined
    endif;
    -- This lazy rule is executed when called by the previous rule to copy an
     -- ownedAttribute property with its upper, lower, and default
     -- multiplicity values to the target model
lazy rule Attribute{
    from
            s : UML!Property
    to
            t : UML!Property(name <- s.name, type <- s.type,
     upperValue<-thisModule.LiteralUnlimitedNatural(s.upperValue),
     lowerValue <- thisModule.LiteralInteger(s.lowerValue),
     defaultValue <- thisModule.LiteralString(s.defaultValue)) }
```

```
        -- This lazy rule is called by the previous rule to copy a memberEnd
        -- property with its upper and lower multiplicity values to the target
        -- model as well as copy the association attached to it by calling the
        -- lazy rule Association
lazy rule Property{
        from
                s : UML!Property
        to
                t : UML!Property(name <- s.name, type <- s.type,
                association <- thisModule.Association(s.association),
         upperValue<-thisModule.LiteralUnlimitedNatural(s.upperValue),
         lowerValue <- thisModule.LiteralInteger(s.lowerValue)) }
        -- This lazy rule is executed when called by the previous rule to copy
        -- the Association and its ownedEnd and memberEnd to the target model
unique lazy rule Association{
        from
                s : UML!Association
        to
                t : UML!Association(name<-s.name,ownedEnd<-s.ownedEnd,
                        memberEnd <- s.memberEnd) }
```

Properties related to a class (attributes), generalizations, and operations are elements contained into a class, so according to the UML containment hierarchies they are selected whenever their container is selected. The use case diagram is generated similarly to the class diagram (see [Tawhid & Petriu, 2011a] for more details).

After generating a specific product model, the generic performance specifications annotating it need to be bound to concrete values. The transformation collects from the generated UML product model all the generic performance parameters and all the PC-features from the PC-feature model, and associates each PC-feature to its corresponding model element(s). For instance, the PC-feature *dataCompression* is associated to a model element of type *message,* since it has an impact on the message size and the communication overheads. The transformation generates spreadsheets containing all the attributes that need binding, as seen in the following example.

```
        -- Rule Message2Row collects all the generic tagged values of the
        -- stereotypes «PaStep» or «PaCommStep» that annotate model element of
        -- type message and transforms them to a row in a table
rule Message2Row {
        from
                s : UML!Message (s.hasStereotype('PaStep')or
                                s.hasStereotype('PaCommStep'))
        using {hostDemand_name : Sequence(String) = Sequence {
                'Message', s.name, 'PaStep', 'hostDemand',
                s.getAttrValue('PaStep','hostDemand').first()};
         msgSize_name : Sequence(String) = Sequence {
                'Message', s.name, 'PaCommStep', 'msgSize',
                s.getAttrValue('PaCommStep','msgSize').first()};}        to
        hostDemand_row : Table!Row(
```

```
cells <- Sequence{ hostDemand_cols }),
hostDemand_cols : distinct Table!Cell foreach(name in
hostDemand_name) (content <- name ),
msgSize_row : Table!Row(
cells <- Sequence{ msgSize_cols }),
msgSize_cols : distinct Table!Cell foreach(name in
 msgSize_name) (content <- name)}
```

Element Type	Element Name	Stereotype Name	Attribute Name	PC-Feature Group Name	PC-Feature Name	Guideline for Value	Generic Parameter	Concrete Value
Message	requisitionRequest	PaStep	hostDemand	application-annotation			$ReqSD (ms)	
		PaCommStep	msgSize	«exactly-one-of feature» dataCompression	compressed	msgSize reduced 10% ...30%		
					uncompressed	No effect		
							$MReq (KB)	
			commTxOvh	«exactly-one-of feature» secureCommunicatio	unsecured	No effect		
					secured			
				«exactly-one-of feature» secured	SSL Protocol			
					TLS Protocol			
				«exactly-one-of feature» securityLevel	lowSecurity	commTxOvh increased 5% ... 25%		
					mediumSecurity	commTxOvh increased 10% ... 35%		
					highSecurity	commTxOvh increased 15% ... 45%		
				«exactly-one-of feature» dataCompression	compressed	commTxOvh increased 2% ...5%		
					uncompressed	No effect		
							$MReqS(ms/KB)	
			commRcvOvh	«exactly-one-of feature» secureCommunicatio	unsecured	No effect		
					secured			
				«exactly-one-of feature» secured	SSL Protocol			
					TLS Protocol			
				«exactly-one-of feature» securityLevel	lowSecurity	commRcvOvh increased 5% ... 25%		
					mediumSecurity	commRcvOvh increased 10% ... 35%		
					highSecurity	commRcvOvh increased 15% ... 45%		
				«exactly-one-of feature» dataCompression	compressed	commRcvOvh increased 2% ...5%		
					uncompressed	No effect		
							$MReqRcv(ms/KB)	

Fig. 7. Part of the generated Spreadsheet *for the scenario* Create Requisition

A part of the generated spreadsheet for the scenario *Create Requisition* is shown in Fig. 7. For instance, the PC-feature *dataCompression* is mapped to message size through the MARTE attribute *msgSize* annotating a model element of type *message*. The column titled *Concrete Value* is designated for the user to enter the concrete value for each corresponding generic parameter, while the column *Guideline for Value* provides a typical range of values to guide the user. The generated spreadsheet presents a user-friendly format for the users of the transformation who have to provide appropriate concrete values for binding the generic SPL annotation variables.

Another kind of mapping that takes place is that of the generic processing nodes from the SPL deployment diagram to actual nodes for a specific product. Each lifeline in the sequence diagrams is stereotyped as «PaRunTInstance», providing an explicit connection at the annotation level between a role in a behaviour definition (a lifeline) and the corresponding runtime instance of an active object (process or thread), whose tag {host=$CustNode} indicates the physical node from the deployment diagram on which the instance is running. Thus, this tag needs to be bound to a concrete node for the product. The generated product model has either a centralized or distributed deployment diagram with maximum numbers of processors. The transformation collects all these processors' name and associates a list of these processors to each lifeline in the spreadsheets. The user will indicate a specific processor from this list.

After the user enters concrete values for all the generic performance parameters and selects an actual processor for each lifeline role provided in the spreadsheets, the second part of the model transformation takes as input these spreadsheets along with its corresponding product model, and binds all the generic MARTE tagged values in the product to the specific values provided in the spreadsheets. The outcome of this part of the transformation is a specific product model with concrete performance annotations for a specific PC-feature configuration, which can be further transformed automatically into a performance model.

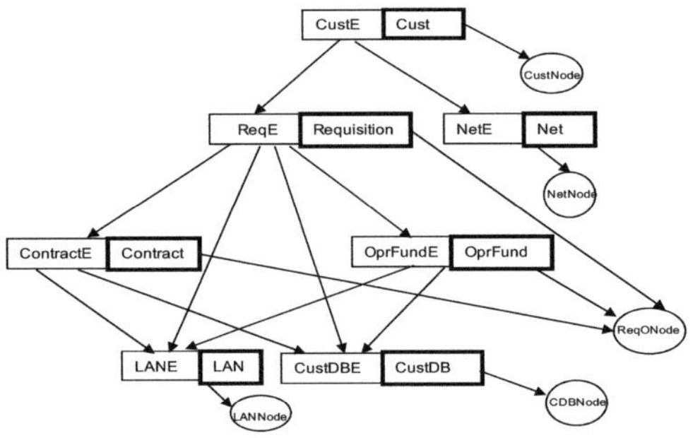

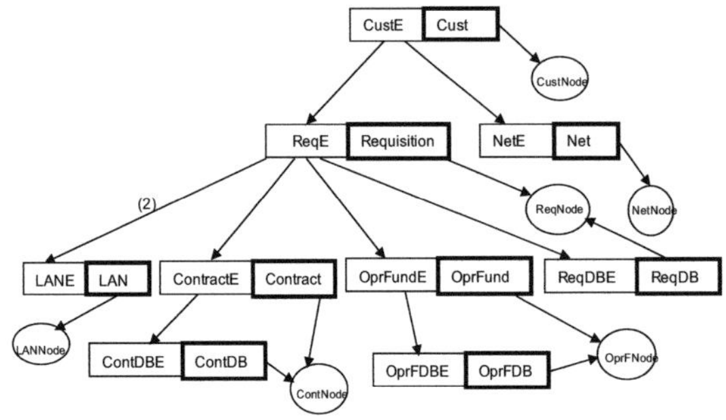

Fig. 8. Centralized LQN model Fig. 9. Distributed LQN model

5. Performance analysis

As mentioned before, the derivation of a performance model from a SPL model requires two model transformations. The first transformation from the annotated SPL model to a product model with concrete performance annotations while the second one takes the target model of a concrete product and transforms it into a LQN performance model using the PUMA transformation approach [Woodside et al., 2005]. This section presents an example of an LQN performance model for the scenario *Create Requisition* shown in Fig.5 of a specific B2B system runs on two different architectures (centralized and distributed). Some performance analysis experiments conducted with the LQN models obtained for a concrete B2B system with a given PC-feature configuration is presented as well.

5.1 Performance model

The LQN model [Xu et al., 2003] is an extension of the well-known Queueing Network model developed for modelling software systems, which able to represent nested services. A software server often requires services from other servers in order to fulfil the requests of its own clients. An LQN model consists of a set of tasks that offer services represented by entries. The entries of a task may send requests to entries of other tasks. Software components are mapped to tasks while hardware devices mapped to hosts. Graphically, the software tasks are depicted as thick rectangles and the entries with attached thin rectangles. The hardware devices are represented as ellipses. LQN is used to model several types of system behaviour and inter-process communication style.

After obtaining the target model of a concrete product, it will be transformed into a LQN performance model using the PUMA transformation [Woodside et al., 2005]. The key performance scenario *Create Requisition* is transformed into two LQN models shown in Fig.8 and Fig.9 to represent the two different architectures; centralized and distributed, respectively. In the centralized architecture, all customer database is allocated to the node *CDBNode* while, in the distributed architecture, the customer information is distributed over the three nodes *ReqNode, ContNode,* and *OprFNode.*

5.2 Performance results

Web-based applications, such as an e-commerce system that contains sensitive data and has many customers, require securing the data transmitted over certain communication channels. However, adding security may include a performance price. System designers need to make choices between different security levels and to make security/performance trade-offs. At the same time, it is important where the data is located in order to fulfill performance and security requirements. This location problem is examined in two different architectures: 1) distributed and 2) centralized. In the centralized architecture, all customer data is contained in one database. The centralized architecture has the advantage that updating and maintaining the data consistency is easier, but has the disadvantage of becoming the system bottleneck for large system sizes (when both the number of customers and the amount of data go up). A distributed architecture represents a solution where several databases divide the data and the work among them. It has potential for faster response times and improved performance, but makes the updates and keeping data consistency more difficult.

In order to illustrate the impact on performance of a secure communication channel between the browser and the webServer, a performance analysis experiment based on LQN models derived for B2B systems with different security levels running on two different architectures (centralized and distributed) is presented.

When a B2B system is generated, a specific configuration has to be selected from the PC-feature model. The key performance scenario *Create Requisition* in Fig. 5 is transformed into the LQN models shown in Fig. 8 and Fig. 9 used for experiments. Two configurations were chosen. The first configuration is for the centralized architecture where the customer database is running on the node *CDBNode* while the roles *Requisition, Contracts,* and *OperationFund* are running on the same node *ReqONode* as shown in Fig. 8. Furthermore, this node is linked to the *CDBNode* through a Local Area Network (LAN) channel with 1.0 ms latency. The connection between the *CustNode* and the *ReqONode* is set up through DSL Internet channels with 100 ms latency. The data is transmitted uncompressed with an average message size of 377.6 KB. The *CustomerAccount* database accesses an external device (hard disk) with an average read/write time of 77.1 ms. The second configuration is for the distributed architecture where the roles *RequisitionDB, ContDB,* and *OpFundDB* are running on the different nodes *ReqNode, contNode,* and *optFNode,* respectively as shown in Fig. 9. These nodes are connected through a LAN channel with 1.0 ms latency.

All communication channels in the unsecure system include no security solution, while the secure system contains certain secure channels using the TLS protocol. TLS has two phases: the handshake phase is used by the browser and webServer to exchange secrets and to generate a confidential symmetric key that is used for data exchange during data transfer, the second phase of the protocol. The public key encryption in the handshake phase may use keys of different lengths; a longer key provides a higher level of security, but the performance overhead increases. The strength of the symmetric encryption key and message digest algorithms used by technology to exchange data may also vary, using strong encryption and authentication algorithms providing higher security. These algorithms are computationally intensive and add different performance overheads to the system. We used the data provided in [Menasce et al., 2004] for performance attribute values, which were obtained from measurements for three levels of security: the handshake overhead is of 10.2ms, 23.8 ms, 48.0 ms, and the data transfer overhead per KB of data is of 0.104 ms, 0.268 ms, 0.609 ms. The fourth case is for an unsecure system.

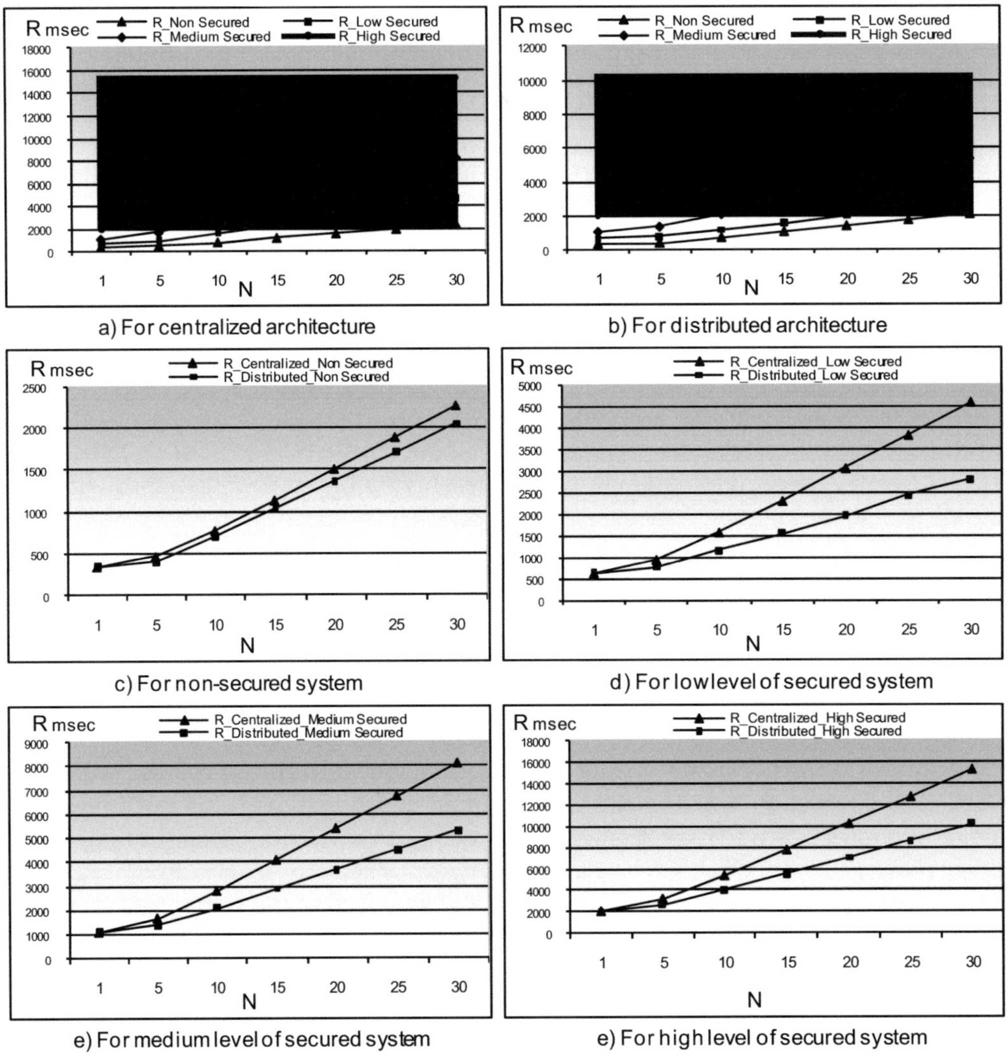

Fig. 10. Response time in function of the number of users

The LQN performance model is analyzed for different numbers of users with an existing solver [Franks, 2000]. Fig. 10a shows the response time of a user creating a requisition for different system choices (unsecure system and three security levels) running on centralized architecture, while Fig. 10b shows the same for a distributed architecture. Fig. 10c-f show the response time in function of the number of simultaneous users executing the same scenario and running on the two different architectures for different levels of security.

The LQN results show that the secure system has a considerable effect on performance, as the response time for the secure system is much higher than for the unsecure system. As the number of users increases, the response time increases significantly due to the competition for resources. The *dataStorage* feature which is centralized or distributed has also a significant effect on performance, as the response time for the centralized architecture is significantly higher than for the distributed architecture for all levels of security.

This brief example illustrates the potential for performance analysis in early development stages, by allowing developers to analyze trade-off between two non-functional requirements, performance and security, and to compare the impacts of different design alternatives on performance. In general, a quantitative performance model helps the analyst to verify whether a system has the capacity to meet its performance requirements. It also helps indentifying the performance "hot spots" (e.g., the resources that will saturate first) and provides guidance for design or configuration changes in order to solve or mitigate the problems.

6. Conclusions

In this chapter, we propose to integrate performance analysis in the early phases of SPL model-driven development process. The goal is to help developers to evaluate the system performance and to choose better design alternatives as early as possible, so that the systems being built will meet their performance requirements. We start with a multi-view UML model of core family assets representing the commonality and variability between different products, which we call the SPL model. We add another dimension to the SPL model, annotating it with generic performance specifications expressed in the standard UML profile MARTE. A first model transformation derives the UML model of a specific product with concrete MARTE performance annotations from the SPL model. A second transformation generates a Layered Queueing Network performance model for the given product by applying an existing transformation approach named PUMA, developed in previous work. To the best of our knowledge, our research is the first to tackle the problem of generating a performance model for a specific product out of the SPL model. The main research challenges are rooted in the fact that a SPL model does not represent a uniquely defined system that could be implemented, run and measured as a whole, so we cannot talk about analyzing the SPL performance. A SPL model is instead a collection of core, generic asset models, which are building blocks for many different products with all kind of options and alternatives. Hence, we need to derive first a given product model with concrete performance-related details, and then we can consider transforming it into a performance model that can be used for performance analysis.

An important factor that distinguishes the SPL development from traditional software systems is variability modeling, a means of expressing the criteria that differentiate between SPL members. Different approaches for variability modeling have been proposed in literature, based on different concepts such as: features, variation points and variants, use case diagrams, or choices and decisions. Our approach employs the feature model to represent variability between the family members, but we have also extended the use of features to express variability in performance completions.

We have considered developing a user-friendly approach. First, a mapping technique for explicit and implicit mapping of features to model elements is proposed, which aims to reduce the clutter of variability specifications in the SPL design model. Secondly, dealing manually with a huge number of generic performance annotations, by asking the developer to inspect every diagram in the model to extract these annotations in order to provide concrete binding values is an error-prone process. In this research, we automate the process of collecting all the generic parameters from the annotated UML model and present them in a user-friendly format to the user.

7. Acknowledgment

This research was partially supported by Discovery grant from the Natural Sciences and Engineering Research Council of Canada (NSERC) and by the Centre of Excellence for Research in Adaptive Systems (CERAS).

8. References

Atlas Transformation Language (ATL), www.eclipse.org/m2m/atl

Bartholdt, J., Medak, M. & Oberhauser, R. (2009). Integrating Quality Modeling with Feature Modeling in Software Product Lines, *Proceedings of the 4th International Conference on Software Engineering Advances* (ICSEA2009), pp.365-370, 2009.

Belategi, L., Sagardui, G. & Etxeberria, L. (2010). Variability Management in Embedded Product Line Analysis, *Proceedings of the 2nd International Conference on Advances in System Testing and Validation Lifecycle* (VALID'10), pp. 69-74, Nice, France, 2010.

Belategi, L., Sagardui, G. & Etxeberria, L. (2010). MARTE mechanisms to model variability when analyzing embedded software product Lines, *Proceedings of the 14th International Conference on Software Product Line* (SPLC'10), pp.466-470, 2010.

Belategi, L., Sagardui, G. & Etxeberria, L. (2011). Model based analysis process for embedded software product lines, *Proceedings of the 2011 International Conference on Software and Systems Process* (ICSSP '11), 2011.

Botterweck, G., Lee, K. & Thiel, S. (2009). Automating Product Derivation in Software Product Line Engineering, *Proceedings of Software Engineering 2009* (SE09), pp 177-182, Kaiserslautern, Germany, 2009.

Clements, P. C. & Northrop, L. M. (2001). *Software Product Lines: Practices and Products*, Addison Wesley.

Cortellessa, V., Di Marco, A. & Inverardi, P. (2007). Non-Functional Modeling and Validation in Model-Driven Architecture, *Proceedings of the 6th Working IEEE/IFIP Conference on Software Architecture* (WICSA07), pp. 25, Mumbai, 2007.

Czarnecki, K. & Antkiewicz, M. (2005). Mapping Features to Models: A Template Approach Based on Superimposed Variants, *Proceedings of the 4th international conference on Generative Programming and Component Engineering* (GPCE), LNCS vol. 3676, pp. 422–437, Springer, 2005.

Czarnecki, K., Antkiewicz, M., Kim, C.H.P., Lau S. & Pietroszek, K. (2005). Model-Driven Software Product Lines, *Proceedings of the Object Oriented Programming Systems Languages and Applications conference*, OOPSLA, San Diego, California, 2005.

Czarnecki, K., Helsen, S. & Eisenecker, U. (2005). Formalizing cardinality-based feature models and their specialization, Software Process Improvement and Practice, pp. 7–29, 2005.

Franks, G. (2000). Performance Analysis of Distributed Server Systems, Report OCIEE-00-01, PhD. thesis, Carleton University, 2000.

Gamez, N. and Fuentes, L. (2011). Software Product Line Evolution with Cardinality-based Feature Models, *Proceedings of the 12th International conference on Software reuse* (ICSR 2011), pp. 102-118, 2011.

Gomaa, H. (2005). *Designing Software Product Lines with UML: From Use Cases to Pattern-based Software Architectures*, Addison-Wesley Object Technology Series, July 2005.

Groher, I. & Voelter, M. (2009). Aspect-Oriented Model-Driven Software Product Line Engineering, *Transactions on Aspect-Oriented Software Development* (AOSD) VI, LNCS, pp. 111-152, 2009.

Happe, J., Becker, S., Rathfelder, C., Friedrich, H. & Reussner, R. H. (2010). Parametric performance completions for model-driven performance prediction, Performance Evaluation, Volume 67 , Issue 8, pp. 694-716, 2010.

Heidenreich, F. &Wende, C. (2007). Bridging the Gap between Features and Models, *Proceedings of the 2nd Workshop on Aspect-Oriented Product Line Engineering* (AOPLE07) co-located with the 6th International Conference on Generative Programming and Component Engineering (GPCE"07), 2007.

Heidenreich, F., Kopcsek, J. & Wende, C. (2008). FeatureMapper: Mapping Features to Models, *Proceedings of the 30th International Conference on Software Engineering* (ICSE08), pp. 943-944, New York, NY, USA, 2008.

Istoan, P., Biri, N. & Klein, J. (2011). Issues in Model-Driven Behavioural Product Derivation, *Proceedings of 5th International Workshop on Variability Modelling of Software-intensive Systems* (Vamos 2011), ACM, p. 69-78, Namur, Belgium, 2011.

Menasce, D., Almeida, V. & Dowdy, L. (2004). *Performance by Design: Computer Capacity Planning by Example*, Prentice Hall PTR, Upper Saddle River, NJ 07458, 2004.

Object Management Group, "UML: Super-structure", Version 2.1.2, OMG document formal/2007-11-02, 2007.

Object Management Group (2011). UML Profile for Modeling and Analysis of Real-Time and Embedded Systems (MARTE),Version 1.1, OMG document formal/2011-06-02, 2011.

Raatikainen, M., Niemelä, E., Myllärniemi, V. & Männistö, T. (2008). Svamp - An Integrated Approach for Modeling Functional and Quality Variability, *Proceedings of the 2nd International Workshop on Variability Modeling of Software-intensive Systems* (VaMoS), 2008.

Stoiber, R. & Glinz, M. (2009). Modeling and Managing Tacit Product Line Requirements Knowledge, *Proceedings of the 2nd Interna-tional Workshop on Managing Requirements Knowledge* (MaRK09), at RE'09, Atlanta, USA, 2009.

Street, J. & Gomaa, H. (2006). An Approach to Performance Modeling of Software Product Lines, *Workshop on Modeling and Analysis of Real-Time and Embedded Systems*, Genova, Italy, October 2006.

Tawhid, R. & Petriu, D.C. (2008). Towards Automatic Derivation of a Product Performance Model from a UML Software Product Line Model, *Proceedings of the 2008 ACM Int. Work-shop on Software Performance* (WOSP08), pp. 91-102, 2008.

Tawhid, R. & Petriu, D.C. (2008). Integrating Performance Analysis in the Model Driven Development of Software Product Lines, *Proceedings of MODELS* 2008, LNCS Vol. 5301, pp. 490-504, 2008.

Tawhid, R. & Petriu, D.C. (2011). Product Model Derivation by Model Transformation in Soltware Product Lines, *Proc. 2nd IEEE Workshop on Model-based Engineering for Real-Time Embedded Systems* (MoBE-RTES 2011), Newport Beach, CA, USA, 2011.

Tawhid, R. & Petriu, D.C. (2011). Automatic Derivation of a Product Performance Model from a Software Product Line Model, *Proceedings of the 15th International Conference on Software Product Line* (SPLC'11), Munich, Germany, 2011.

Woodside, M., Petriu, D. C. & Siddiqui, K. H. (2002). Performance-related Completions for Software Specifications, *Proceedings of the 22rd International Conference on Software Engineering*, ICSE 2002, pp. 22-32, Orlando, Florida, USA, 2002.

Woodside, M., Petriu, D.C., Petriu, D.B., Shen, H., Israr, T. & Merseguer, J. (2005). Performance by Unified Model Analysis (PUMA), *Proceedings of the 5th ACM Int.Workshop on Software and Performance WOSP'2005*, pp. 1-12, Palma, Spain, 2005.

Xu, J., Woodside, C.M. & Petriu D.C. (2003). Performance Analysis of a Software Design using the UML Profile for Schedulability, Performance and Time, *TOOLS'2003, (P.Kemper and W.Sanders, eds.)* Springer LNCS Vol. 2794, pp.291-307, 2003.

5

Defects in Product Line Models and How to Identify Them

Camille Salinesi and Raúl Mazo
CRI, Panthéon Sorbonne University
France

1. Introduction

The history of software and system development shows that abstraction plays a major role in making complexity manageable (Bosch 2000). Thus, abstracting the common and variable artefacts of an undefined collection of products and organising them into a model may be a good option to manage the complexity of a product line. Product line models improve decision-making processes. In addition, the representation of PLMs in different views improves communication of the actors participating in the product line management (Finkelstein et al. 1992). Nuseibeh et al. (1994) describe views as partial representations of a system and its domain.

Several approaches have been found in literature to represent commonality and variability of a product line. Most of the approaches use features (Kang et al. 1990) as the central concept of product line models. However, other modelling approaches exist like Orthogonal Variability Models (OVM, cf. Pohl et al. 2005), Dopler variability models (Dhungana et al. 2010), Textual Variability Language (TVL, cf. Boucher et al. 2010 and Classen et al. 2010), and constraint-based product line language (Djebbi et al. 2007, Mazo *et al.* 2011e; Salinesi *et al.* 2010b; 2011).

Quality assurance of PLMs has recently been a prominent topic for researchers and practitioners in the context of product lines. Identification and correction of PLMs defects, is vital for efficient management and exploitation of the product line. Defects that are not identified or not corrected will inevitably spread to the products created from the product line, which can drastically diminish the benefits of the product line approach (Von der Maßen and Lichter 2004, Benavides 2007). Besides, product line modeling is an error-prone activity. Indeed, a product line specification represents not one, but an undefined collection of products that may even fulfil contradictory requirements (Lauenroth *et al.* 2010). The aforementioned problems enforce the urgent need of early identification and correction of defects in the context of product lines.

Product line models quality has been an intensive research topic over the last ten years (Von der Maßen & Lichter 2004; Zhang *et al.* 2004; Batory 2005; Czarnecki & Pietroszek 2006; Benavides 2007; Janota & Kiniry 2007; Lauenroth & Pohl 2007; Trinidad *et al.* 2008; Van den Broek & Galvão 2009; Elfaki *et al.* 2009; Kim *et al.* 2011; Liu *et al.* 2011). Usually, to guaranty a certain level of quality of a model, this one must be verified against a collection of criteria and then, these defects must be corrected. Verifying PLMs entails finding undesirable properties, such as redundancies, anomalies or inconsistencies (Von der Maßen *et al.* 2004). It is widely accepted that manual verification is already tedious and error-prone (Benavides *et al.* 2005). This is even worst when several (often millions) of products are represented altogether in a single specification. Several approaches to automate verification of PLMs have been proposed in order to overcome this limitation. However, despite the relative success of these approaches, there is still a number of pending issues that have motivated the proposal developed in this chapter:

1. Quality assurance techniques from the development of single systems cannot be directly applied to product line specifications because these specifications contain variability. As shows the example presented by Lauenroth *et al.* (2010), a product line may contain requirements R and $\neg R$ at the same time. When a traditional technique is used for verifying this specification, even though those requirements are not included for the same product, a contradiction would be identified since the requirements R and $\neg R$ cannot be fulfilled together. Therefore, it is necessary to take into account the variability of the product line to check whether contradictory requirements can really be part of the same product.
2. The current state of the art on verification is mainly focused on feature models (Kang et al. 1990). Only properties that can be evaluated over feature models represented as boolean expressions are considered in these works. This brushes aside the non-boolean elements of the more sophisticated product line specification formalisms (e.g., integer cardinalities, attributes and complex constraints; cf. Mazo et al. 2011d, Salinesi et al. 2010b, 2011). Current approaches restrict the verification operations to those that can be solved by boolean solvers. The verification is guided by the pre-selected technology and not by the verification requirements themselves. As a result, verification techniques are designed for a limited number of formalisms. These verification techniques are inadequate for many of the existing formalisms, included some used in an industrial context (Djebbi *et al.* 2007; Dhungana *et al.* 2010).
3. Inadequate support for multi-model specification. The size and complexity of industrial product line models motivates the development of this one by heterogeneous teams (Dhungana *et al.* 2006; Segura 2008). Nevertheless, existing tools provide only little support for integrating the models developed by different teams and the subsequent verification of the global model and configurations of products from that model. For instance, a global model that integrates two models must itself have no defects resulting from the integration.

Also in the context of PLs specified with several models, we have identified in our literature review a weak support for verifying the global view of the product line. A product line model has to change over time and in multi-model PLs a change on one of the models can make the global view inconsistent. To the best of our knowledge, existing tools do not provide automated mechanisms for detecting errors on the global PLM as a result of the changes in the different models of the PLM.

This chapter addresses the fourth problem situations aforementioned. To tackle these situations, we present in Section 2 the most relevant concepts used in this chapter, a literature review of related works and the running example to be used in the rest of the chapter. Section 3 presents our typology of verification criteria, which is developed in

Section 4 for the case of single-view product line models, and Section 5 for the case of multi-view product line models. Section 6 presents the evaluation of the approach presented in this chapter.

2. Background and running example

This section presents a literature review on verification of product line models and the corresponding analysis regarding the gaps and challenges identified in each approach. This section also presents a UNIX product line and the corresponding model of the whole or a part of the PL in three different PL modeling languages. The UNIX PL will be used in the rest of this chapter as our running example.

2.1 Verification of product line models

Verifying PLMs entails several aspects. On the one hand, a product line model, independently of the language used to express it, must respect certain properties associated with the domain of product lines. On the other hand, certain properties are associated with the concepts used in the language in which it is expressed. Therefore, some properties of PLMs are independent of the language while other ones are particular to each language. Thus, product line models can be verified from two different points of view. This chapter proposes an approach for PLM verification (Von der Maßen & Lichter 2004; Lauenroth & Pohl 2007; Mendonça *et al.* 2009) in with the engineer selects the verification operations that he/she want to use according to the language in which the model(s) to be verified are specified. In this approach, verification consists in "finding undesirable properties, such as redundant or contradictory information" (Trinidad *et al.* 2008). For instance, PLMs should not be void (i.e., they should allow to configure more than one product) and for the languages with the concept of *optionality*, elements modeled as optional must be really optional (i.e., they should not appear in all the products configured from the PLM).

2.2 Related work

Von der Maßen & Lichter (2004) present an approach to identify redundancies, anomalies and inconsistencies. According to the authors, a feature model contains redundancy, "if at least one semantic information is modeled in a multiple way"; anomalies, "if potential configurations are being lost, though these configurations should be possible"; and inconsistencies, "if the model includes contradictory information". Several cases of redundancies, anomalies and inconsistencies on FMs are identified. In order to validate the approach, the authors use RequiLine, a tool that allows detecting inconsistencies on the domain and on the product configuration level (Von der Maßen & Lichter 2003). The approach was evaluated in "a small local software company" and "in a global player of the automotive industry". However no information about the automating detection of redundancies and anomalies, no details about the sizes of the models or about the technology used to automate the approach or about the results obtained were provided.

Whereas Batory (2005) used grammar and propositional formulas to represent basic FMs and enable truth maintenance systems and SAT solvers to identify contradictory (or inconsistency) predicates to verify that a given combination of features effectively defines a product. In the same line as Batory, Hemakumar (2008) proposed a dynamic solution to find contradictions, "where errors can be detected during usage and silently reported to model designers". The author proposes an incremental consistency algorithm that incrementally verifies some contradiction properties. The approach consists in verify that a model is contradiction-free if it is k-contradiction free for all k where $0<k\leq n$ (A feature model is k-contradiction free if every selection of k features does not expose a contradiction, for example: "unconditionally" dead features are exposed when $k=1$). When $k=n$, where n is the number of user selectable features, the model has been proven to be contradiction free. However, the incremental consistency algorithm has important practical limits because it is limited to "verify contradiction freedom of models with about 20 or fewer features".

In (Benavides *et al.* 2005a; 2005b; 2006; 2007; Trinidad *et al.* 2008), authors transform FODA models with and without attributes into Boolean expressions. These expressions are executed on Constraint Satisfaction Problem (CSP), Satisfiability (SAT) and Binary Decision Diagrams (BDD) solvers in order to execute analysis and verification operations over feature models. In (Benavides *et al.* 2006) the relationships of the FM are represented as *ifThenElse* constrains on CPS. Despite the originality of this proposal, the constraint representing a feature cardinality (*m,n*) between the father feature *A* and its child *B* (according to their notation: *ifThenElse(A=0;B=0;B in {n,m})*) does not consider that the feature *A* can itself have a feature cardinality, and in this case the semantic of feature cardinalities is not well represented in the constraint. Authors performed a comparative test between two off-the-shelf CSP Java solvers (JaCoP and Choco). The experiment was executed on five FMs with up to 52 features and in both solvers. The time to get one solution seemed to be linear and the time to get all solutions seemed to be exponential.

Janota & Kiniry (2007) have formalized in higher-order logic (HOL) a "feature model meta-model" that integrates properties of several feature modeling approaches such as attributes and cardinalities. Once the model represented in HOL, author have formulated HOL expressions for root selectivity, existence of a path of selected features from the root to a feature that has been selected, and cardinality satisfaction of a selected feature that each feature model must respect. The approach has been implemented in *Mobius program verification environment*, an Eclipse-based platform for designing, testing, performing various kinds of verification of Java programs and bytecode. Nevertheless, the paper does not provide evidence about the evaluation of the approach, its scalability and its applicability to real cases.

Trinidad *et al.* (2008) mapped FMs into CSP in order to find and diagnose three types of errors: (i) "dead features" are non-selectable features (features that do not appear in any product); (ii) "false optional features", which are features that in spite of being modeled as optional, are always chosen whenever their parents are chosen; and (iii) "void models";a feature model is said to be void if no product can be defined from it. The goal of Trinidad et al. is to detect the above three errors and provide explanations for the cause of these errors. In order to achieve the first goal, authors transform the FM into a CSP expression and then, to query the Choco solver (by means of the FaMa tool) to find the errors. The approach has been evaluated on five FMs up to 86 features. Unfortunately, no details about the scalability and the efficiency of the approach and tool are provided.

Van der Storm (2007) transformed feature diagrams into BDDs in order to check configurations, obtain valid configurations and check consistency of the feature diagram.

Checking the consistency of the feature diagram consists in checking the satisfiability for the BDD logical formulas. Unfortunately, neither details about implementation nor performance nor scalability of the approach are provided in the paper.

Yan et al. (2009) proposed an approach that consists in eliminating verification-irrelevant features and constraints from FMs in order to reduce the problem size of verification, and alleviate the state-space explosion problem. The authors carried out an experiment in which they generated FMs with up to 1900 features. The authors verified the consistency of models and showed that verification is faster when the redundant features had been eliminated. The problem with this approach is that it only considers as redundant, the constraints that contain redundant features, whereas it does not consider typical redundancies such as domain overlapping or cyclic relationships (Salinesi *et al.* 2010; Mazo *et al.* 2011). Besides, (i) the validation of the approach was done with in-house and random build features models, which does not guaranty that the approach works with real world feature models; and (ii) the details about the formalisation and implementation of the approach are not revealed.

Van den Broek & Galvão (2009) analyze FODA product line models using generalized feature trees. In their approach they translate FMs into feature trees plus additional constraints. Once FMs represented in the functional programming language Miranda, they detect the existence of products (void models), dead features and minimal set of conflicting constraints. In FMs with cross-tree constraints, the function to find the number of products belongs to $O(N*2^M)$, where N is the number of features and M is the number of cross-tree constraints. Unfortunatelly, no evaluation of the theoretical calculations of efficiency is reported in the paper. The approach was validated with a feature tree of 13 features and two cross-tree constraints, which is not enough to evaluate the scalability and the usability of the approach on industrial models.

Elfaki *et al.* (2009) propose to use FOL to detect dead features and inconsistencies due to contradictions between include-type and exclude-type relationships in FMs. The innovative point of their work is the suggestion of expressions dealing with both individuals and sets of features.

SPLOT (Mendonca *et al.* 2009b) is a Web-based reasoning and configuration system for feature models supporting group-cardinalities instead of alternative and or-relations. The system maps feature models into propositional logic formulas and uses boolean-based techniques such as BDD and SAT solvers to verify the validity of models (not void) and find dead features.

2.3 Running example

The example taken in this chapter is that of the UNIX operating system, initially presented in (Mazo *et al.* 2011d). UNIX was first developed in the 1960s, and has been under constant development ever since. As other operating systems, it is a suite of programs that makes computers work. In particular, UNIX is a stable, multi-user and multi-tasking system for many different types of computing devices such as servers, desktops, laptops, down to embedded calculators, routers, or even mobile phones. There are many different versions of UNIX, although they share common similarities. The most popular varieties of UNIX are Sun Solaris, Berkeley (BSD), GNU/Linux, and MacOS X.

The UNIX operating system is made up of three parts: the kernel, the shell and the programs; and two constituent elements: files and processes. Thus, these three parts consist in a collection of files and processes allowing interaction among the parts. The kernel of UNIX is the hub of the operating system: it allocates time and memory to programs and handles the file-store and communications in response to system calls. The shell acts as an interface between the user and the kernel, interprets the commands (programs) typed in by users and arranges for them to be carried out. As an illustration of the way the shell, the programs and the kernel work together, suppose a user types *rm myfile* (which has the effect of removing the file *myfile*). The shell searches the file-store for the file containing the program *rm*, and then requests the kernel, through system calls, to execute the program *rm* on *myfile*. The process *rm* removes *myfile* using a specific system-call. When the process *rm myfile* has finished running, the shell gives the user the possibility to execute further commands.

As for any product line, our example emphasizes the common and variable elements of the UNIX family and the constraints among these elements. This example is built from our experience with UNIX operating systems and it does not pretend to be exhaustive, neither on the constituent elements nor on the constraints among these elements. The idea with this PL is, for instance, to look at what utility programs or what kinds of interfaces are available for a particular user. This PL is composed of the following six constraints:

Constraint 1. UNIX can be installed or not and the installation can be from a CDROM, a USB device or from the NET.

Constraint 2. UNIX provides several hundred UTILITY PROGRAMS for each user. The collection of UTILITY PROGRAMS varies even when the UNIX product is full-configured.

Constraint 3. The SHELL is a kind of UTILITY PROGRAM. Different USERS may use different SHELLS. Initially, each USER has a default shell, which can be overridden or changed by users. Some common SHELLS are:

- Bourne shell (SH)
- TC Shell (TCSH)
- Bourne Again Shell (BASH)

For the sake of simplicity will consider only two users in this running example: ROOT_USER and GUEST_USER.

Constraint 4. Some functions accomplished by the UTILITY PROGRAMS are:

- EDITING (mandatory and requires USER INTERFACE)
- FILE MAINTENANCE (mandatory and requires USER INTERFACE)
- PROGRAMMING SUPPORT (optional and requires USER INTERFACE)
- ONLINE INFO (optional and requires USER INTERFACE)

Constraint 5. The USER INTERFACE can be GRAPHICAL and/or TEXTUAL.

Constraint 6. The GRAPHICAL interface is characterized by a WIDTH RESOLUTION and a HEIGHT RESOLUTION that can have the following couples of values [800,600], [1024,768] and [1366,768].

2.3.1 Representation of the UNIX product line as a feature model

Feature Models (FMs) were first introduced in 1990 as a part of the *Feature-Oriented Domain Analysis (FODA)* method (Kang *et al.* 2002) as a means to represent the commonalities and variabilities of PLs. Since then, feature modeling has become a de facto standard adopted by the software product line community and several extensions have been proposed to improve and enrich their expressiveness. A FM defines the valid combinations of features in a PL, and is depicted as a graph-like structure in which nodes represent features, and edges the relationships between them (Kang *et al.* 2002). Two of these extensions are cardinalities (Riebisch *et al.* 2002; Czarnecki *et al.* 2005) and attributes (Streitferdt *et al.* 2003; White *et al.* 2009). Although there is no consensus on a notation to define attributes, most proposals agree that an attribute is a variable with a name, a domain and a value. Attributes are integers, enumerations, and boolean values representing important properties of a feature; as for instance the price, the cost, the width, the height or the time spent to build the corresponding feature. In this chapter we use the group cardinalities grouping bundles of features (cf. *Cdrom, Usb* and *Net* in Figure 1). We use the semantic of feature models proposed by (Schobbens *et al.* 2007).

The elements of the FM notation used in this chapter are presented and exemplified as follows:

- *Feature*: A feature is a prominent or distinctive user-visible aspect, quality, or characteristic of a software system (Kang *et al.* 1990). For the sake of simplicity FMs usually comport only the name of the feature; for instance Editing in Figure 1. Every FM must have one root, which is called *root feature* and identifies the product line; for example UNIX in Figure 1.
- *Attribute*: Although there is no consensus on a notation to define attributes, most proposals agree that an attribute is a variable with a name (*Name*), a domain (*Domain*), and a value (consistent with the domain) at a given configuration time. From a technical point of view an attribute must to be differentiated from the other ones by an identifier (*IdAttribute*). For instance in Figure 1, *WidthResolution* and *HeightResolution* are two attributes with a domain determined by the constraint at the bottom of the model.
- *Mandatory:* Given two features *F1* and *F2, F1* father of *F2*, a mandatory relationship between *F1* and *F2* means that if the *F1* is selected, then *F2* must be selected too and vice versa. For instance in Figure 1, features *UtilityProgram* and *Editing* are related by a mandatory relationship.
- *Optional:* Given two features *F1* and *F2, F1* father of *F2*, an optional relationship between *F1* and *F2* means that if *F1* is selected then *F2* can be selected or not. However, if *F2* is selected, then *F1* must also be selected. For instance in Figure 1, features *UNIX* and *UtilityProgram* are related by an optional relationship.
- *Requires:* Given two features *F1* and *F2, F1* requires *F2* means that if *F1* is selected in product, then *F2* has to be selected too. Additionally, it means that *F2* can be selected even when *F1* is not. For instance, *Editing* requires *UserInterface* (cf. Figure 1).
- *Exclusion:* Given two features *F1* and *F2, F1* excludes *F2* means that if *F1* is selected then *F2* cannot to be selected in the same product. This relationship is bi-directional: if *F2* is selected, then *F1* cannot to be selected in the same product.
- *Group cardinality:* A group cardinality is an interval denoted <*n..m*>, with *n* as lower bound and *m* as upper bound limiting the number of child features that can be part of a

product when its parent feature is selected. If one of the child features is selected, then the father feature must be selected too. For instance in Figure 1, *Cdrom*, *Usb* and *Net* are related in a *<1..1>* group cardinality.

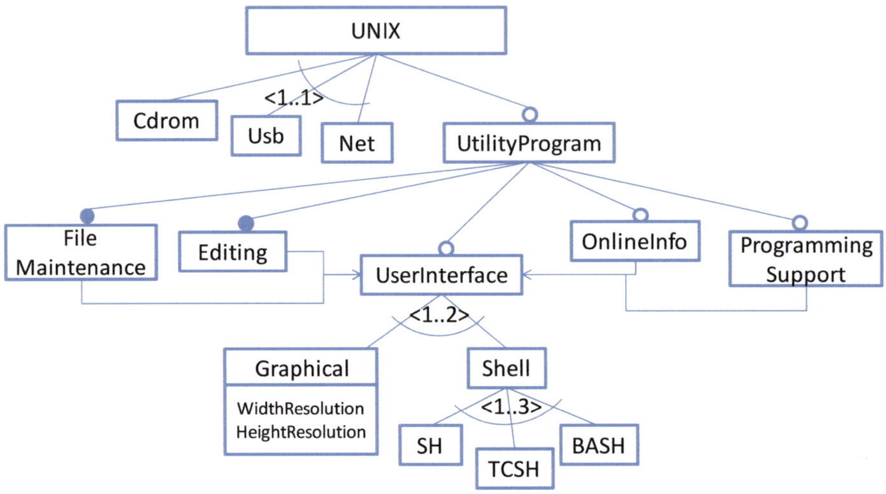

Graphical→ relation([WidthResolution, HeightResolution],{[800, 600], [1024,768], [1366,768]})

Fig. 1. User model of the UNIX operating system family of our running example

Figure 1 corresponds to the feature representation of the user model of our running example. In this model, a user has the possibility to install a UNIX system using one of the following options: a CD ROM, an USB devise or a network. In addition, users have the possibility to install or not utility programs for file maintenance, edition, online access, and user interface. The user interface may be graphical or command-line (Shell) based; there are three options of command-line interface: SH, TCSH and BASH. The utility programs for user interface, online information and programming support are optional features.

2.3.2 Representation of the UNIX product line as a dopler variability model

The Decision-oriented (Dopler) variability modeling language focuses on product derivation and aims at supporting users configuring products. In Dopler variability models (Dhungana *et al.* 2010a; 2010b), the product line's problem space is defined using *decision models* whereas the solution space is specified using *asset models*. An example of Dopler model is presented in Figure 2. This figure depicts the installation of a UNIX operating system (decision model) and the associated packages (asset model) that can be selected if the UNIX system is installed with a graphical interface. The decision model is composed of four decisions. The first one proposes one of three ways to install a UNIX operating system (with a CD ROM, with a USB or with the Net). The solution of this decision implies the solution of a second decision in which the user must select the utility programs to be installed in the particular UNIX system; in that regard, five utility programs are proposed: one tool for editing, one for file maintenance, one for programming, one for online information access and one shell. If the choice contains the utility program for online information, the user must decide what kind of graphical resolution will be configured and several choices are proposed: *800x600*,

1024x768, 1366x768. Depending of each selection, the values of the variables corresponding to the width and height resolution will be assigned automatically by means of several decision effects; for instance in Figure 2: *if(GraphicalResolution==800x600) then Width=800*. To finish, the assignation of the width and height resolution must respect a certain number of validity conditions like for instance: *Width ≥ 800* and *Width ≤ 1366*. The asset model is composed of seven graphical user interfaces and libraries that can be used in a UNIX graphical interface. The *Tab Window Manager* asset is available for all UNIX implementations with a graphical interface and requires the asset *Motif*; the others assets are optional. The IRIS 4d window manager is based on *Mwm* and *Motif* and therefore requires all of them in order to work in the same way as the *KDE* asset requires the *Qt widget toolkit* to work.

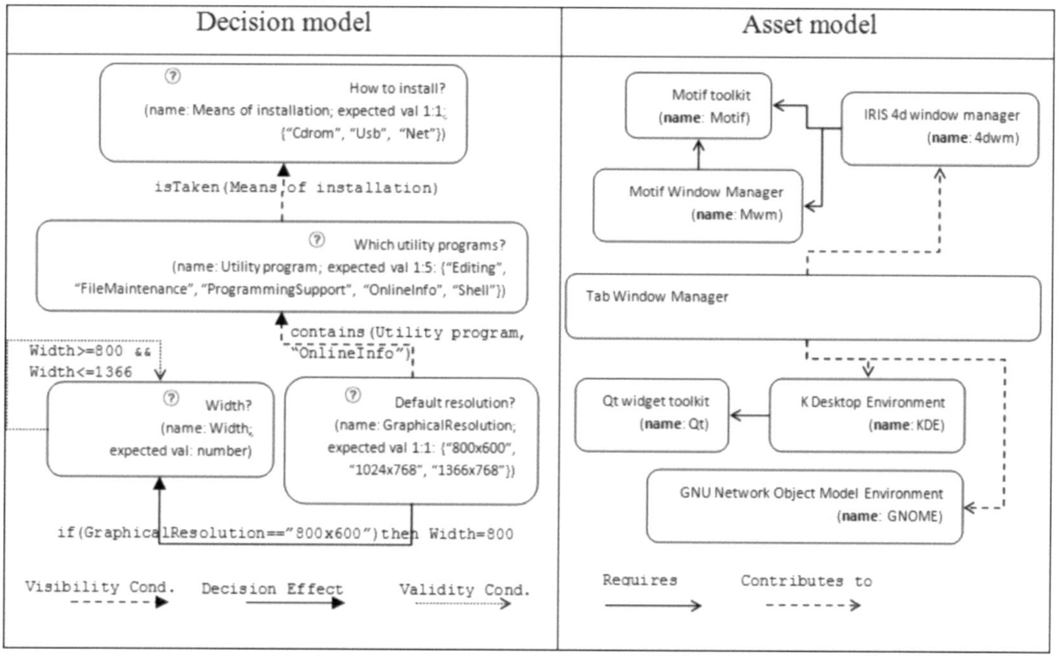

Fig. 2. Example of Dopler Model: Installation of a UNIX System

A **decision model** consists of a set of decisions (e.g., *Which utility programs?* with two attributes: **name** and **expected values**) and dependencies among them (i.e., the **Visibility condition** *isTaken(Means of installation)* forcing the answer of the decision *Utility program* if the decision *Means of installation* is taken). **Assets** allow defining an abstract view of the solution space to the degree of details needed for subsequent product derivation. In a domain-specific metamodel attributes and dependencies can be defined for the different types of assets. Decisions and assets are linked with **inclusion conditions** defining traceability from the solution space to the problem space (e.g., the asset *Tab Window Manager* must be included in the solution space if the option *OnlineInfo* of the decision *Utility program* is selected in a particular configuration). In our integration approach, these inclusion conditions are constraints that will be added to the collection of constraints representing the decision and asset model. Once these constraints are added, both viewpoints of the PL are integrated, and the model is ready to be verified against the typology of verification criteria presented in this chapter.

2.3.3 Representation of the UNIX product line as a constraint program

Constraint Programming (CP) emerged in the 1990's as a successful paradigm to tackle complex combinatorial problems in a declarative manner (Van Hentenryck 1989). CP extends programming languages with the ability to deal with logical variables of different domains (e.g. integers, reals or booleans) and specific declarative relations between these variables called *constraints*. These constraints are solved by specialized algorithms, adapted to their specific domains and therefore much more efficient than generic logic-based engines. A constraint is a logical relationship among several variables, each one taking a value in a given domain of possible values. A constraint thus restricts the possible values that variables can take.

In modern Constraint Programming languages (Diaz & Codognet 2001; Schulte & Stuckey 2008), many different types of constraints exist and are used to represent real-life problems: arithmetic constraints such as $X + Y < Z$, symbolic constraints like *atmost(N,[X1,X2,X3],V)* which means that at most *N* variables among *[X1,X2,X3]* can take the value *V*, global constraints like *alldifferent(X1,X2,…,Xn)*meaning that all variables should have different values, and reified constraints that allow the user to reason about the truth-value of a constraint. Solving constraints consists in first reducing the variable domains by propagation techniques that will eliminate inconsistent value within domains and then finding values for each constrained variable in a labeling phase, that is, iteratively grounding variables (fixing a value for a variable) and propagating its effect onto other variable domains (by applying again the same propagation-based techniques). The labeling phase can be improved by using heuristics concerning the order in which variables are considered as well as the order in which values are tried in the variable domains. Consult (Schulte & Stuckey 2008) for more details. Mazo et al. (2011e) present a constraint system to represent product line models by means of abstract constraints where the domain is an argument of the system.

Our running example can also be represented as a constraint program according to the method proposed by Salinesi et al. (2010; 2011) and Mazo et al. (2011d). The resulting model is presented in the following table, where the first column corresponds to each constraint of our example and the second column its representation as a constraint program.

Constraint	CP Representation
C. 1	UNIX ≤ Cdrom + Usb + Net ≤ UNIX
C. 2	UtilityProgram ≤ UNIX
C. 3	Shell = UtilityProgram ∧ Shell ⇒ ((1 * ROOT_USER ≤ ROOT_USERSH + ROOT_USERTCSH + ROOT_USERBASH ≤ 3 * ROOT_USER) ∧ (1 * GUEST_USER ≤ GUEST_USERSH + GUEST_USERTCSH + GUEST_USERBASH ≤ 3 * GUEST_USER))
C. 4	Editing = UtilityProgram ∧ Editing ⇒ UserInterface ∧ FileMaintenance = UtilityProgram ∧ FileMaintenance ⇒ UserInterface ∧ ProgrammingSupport ≤ UtilityProgram ∧ ProgrammingSupport ⇒ UserInterface ∧

Constraint	CP Representation
	OnlineInfo ≤ UtilityProgram ∧ OnlineInfo ⇒ UserInterface ∧ UserInterface ≤ UtilityProgram
C. 5	1 * UserInterface ≤ Graphical + Textual ≤ 2 * UserInterface
C. 6	Graphical = 1 ⇔ (WidthResolution = W1 ∧ HeightResolution = H1) ∧ Graphical = 0 ⇔ (WidthResolution = 0 ∧ HeightResolution = 0) ∧ relation([W1, H1], [[800, 600], [1024, 768], [1366, 768]])

Table 1. UNIX PL represented as a constraint program

3. Typology of verification criteria

Verifying PLMs entails several aspects. On the one hand, a product line model, independently of the language used to express it, must respect certain properties associated with the domain of product lines. On the other hand, certain properties are associated with the fact that each PLM respects the syntactic rules of the language in which it is expressed. Therefore, some properties of PLMs are independent of the language while other ones are particular to each language. In light of this observation, this chapter proposes a typology of PLM verification criteria adapted from the initial version presented in (Salinesi et al. 2010a). The typology presented in Figure 1 is structure in two levels; the top level represents the three categories of verification criteria and the bottom level represents the corresponding operations of the two criteria with more than one operation. This figure indicates that not all PLM verification criteria are equivalent: some are a result of the specification of the PL with a metamodel, whereas others can be used to verify PL specifications independent of the formalism used when they were specified. Besides, some criteria help verifying the ability of PLM to generate all the desired products and only them, whereas others are interested in the quality of PLMs, independently of their semantics (i.e., the collection of all possible products that can be generated from it). This is for example the case with the respect of certain rules providing formality (i.e., absence of ambiguity) at the PLM.

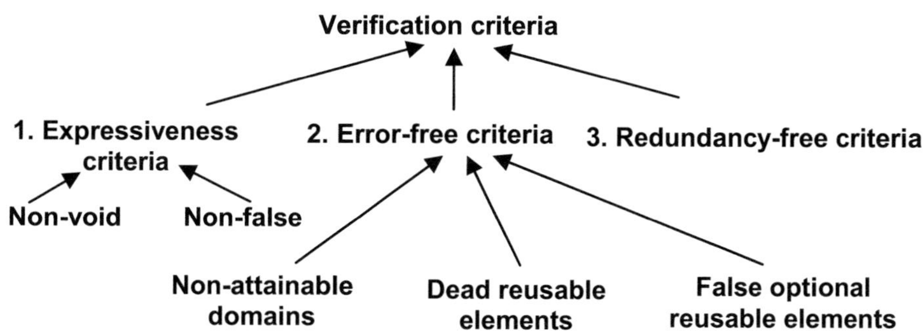

Fig. 3. Typology of verification criteria on PLMs

The outcomes of the typology are multiple:

a. the typology classify the criteria semantic, allowing the identification of similarities and differences among the criteria;
b. the typology makes easier to identify some defects for which no verification criterion is available in the literature. Redundancy of relationships among reusable elements is an example of defect for which no verification criterion has been defined in the literature (at least to our knowledge).
c. the classification behind the typology makes it easier the proposition of a standard and reusable approach to verify the domain-specific criteria of PLMs; and
d. the typology can be used to select the criteria that one wants to use to verify a PLM according to the impact that these criteria have or the expected level of quality of a particular PLM.

The following sections use the typology of verification criteria presented in Figure 3 to develop the verification approach proposed in this chapter.

4. Single-model verification

In order to verify models against the verification criteria identified and calcified in the former section, it is necessary to represent PLMs in a way that is (a) expressiveness-enough to represent the semantics (i.e. the collection of products that can be configured from the PLM) of PLMs, (b) consistent with the formalization of the criteria, and (c) easy to parse with analysis tools. Experience shows that the semantic of every PLM can be represented as a collection of variables over different domains and constrains among these variables. While the variables specify what can vary from a configuration to another one, constraints express under the form of restrictions what combinations of values are allowed in the products.

This section will show how to represent the semantic of PLMs with a constraint based approach, and to verify each and every criterion shown in the typology of the former section on a PLM. The approach will be applied to our feature model example to show how to navigate between the generic specifications of the criteria. The genericity of the approach will be shown by providing examples with other formalisms (cf. Section 5).

Verifying PLMs is about looking for undesirable properties such as redundant or contradictory information. This chapter proposes three domain-specific verification criteria: expressiveness, error-free and redundancy-free. Each domain-specific verification criterion is defined, formalized and exemplified with our running example (cf. Figure 1 and Table 1) as follows.

2.1. Expressiveness: every PLM must allow configuring more than one product, i.e., the model must be not void and the model must be expressive enough to allow configure more than one product (Benavides *et al.* 2005). In case the PLM allows configuring only one product, the PLM, even if it is not considered as a void model, is not expressive enough to be a PLM. Indeed, the purpose of PLMs is to represent at least two products -or there is not reuse. Two verification operations can be used to implement this criterion:

a. **Non-void PLMs**. This operation takes a PLM as input and returns "Void PLM" if the PLM does not define any products. Two alternative techniques have been proposed so far to implement this operation: calculate the number of products (Van den Broek &

Galvão 2009) or ask for a product configuration that meets the constraints of a FM (Benavides *et al.* 2005; Trinidad *et al.* 2008). Our proposal follows along the lines of the latter alternative and is formalized in the following algorithm. It consists in determining if there is at least one product that can be generated by means of a query to an off-the-shelf solver. If the PLM is not void, the solver will return one valid product or *false* otherwise.

```
Non-void _PLM(PLM M, Solver S) {
    S.charge(M);
    Answer = S.getOneSolution();
    If (Answer ≠ "false") {
            Write (Answer);
    }
    Else {
            Write ("Void PLM");
    }
}
```

The execution of this algorithm over the running example gives as result that our UNIX PL is non-void.

b. **Non-false PLMs**. This operation takes a PLM as input and returns "False PLM" if at most one valid product can be configured with it. Although this operation could also help detect when PLMs are void (our precedent operation), the converse is not true. The two operations have then a separate implementation. Our approach consists in asking the solver to generate two products in order to decide if the PLM is false. The algorithm proposed to automate this operation is as follows:

```
Non-false_PLM(PLM M, Solver S) {
    S.charge(M);
    Answer1 = S.getOneSolution();
    If (Answer1 ≠ "false") {
            Answer2 = S.getNextSolution();
            If (Answer2 ≠ "false") {
                    Write (Answer1, Answer2);
            }
            Else {
                    Write ("False PLM");
            }
    }
    Else {
            Write ("False PLM");
    }
}
```

The execution of this algorithm over the running example gives as result that our UNIX PL is a non-false PLM.

2.2. Error-free. The Dictionary of Computing defines an error as "A discrepancy between a computed, observed, or measured value or condition, and the true, specified, or theoretically correct value or condition" (Howe 2010). In PLMs, an error represents a discrepancy between what the engineer want to represent and the result obtained from the model. For instance, this is the case when the engineer includes a new reusable element (in a given domain) in a PLM, but this element never appears in a product. The error-free criterion can be verified by means of three operations: the first one allows identifying the non-attainable domain values of PLM's reusable elements; the second one allows identifying the dead elements, i.e. elements of the PL that are never used in a product; the third one allows identifying the reusable elements modeled as optional but that appear in all the products of the PL. These operations are presented as follows:

c. **Non-attainable domains**: This operation takes a PLM and a collection of reusable elements as input (all of them by default) and returns the reusable elements that cannot attain one of the values of their domain. Reusable elements can have domains represented as particular values (e.g., 800), intervals of values (e.g., [0..5]), or collections of values (e.g., {0, 800, 1024, 1280}). A non-attainable value of a domain is the value of an element that never appears in any product of the product line. For example, if a reusable element R has the domain [0..1], value 1 is non-attainable if R can never be integrated in a product line it never take the value of 1. Non-attainable values are clearly undesired since they give the user a wrong idea about domain of reusable elements. The approach presented in this chapter can assess the attainability of any reusable elements for all (or parts of) their domain values. This operation was also implemented by Trinidad *et al.* (2008), but only for boolean domains on FMs. Our proposal goes a step further by offering an algorithm for any domain as e.g. needed when using attributes or features whit individual cardinality.
Our algorithm to automate this operation evaluates the domain of each variables of the PLM. For each vale of the domain, the algorithm requests the solver at hand for a solution. If the solver gives a solution for all the values of the variable's domain, the variable is erased from the list of reusable elements with non-attainable domains. Otherwise, the variable, representing a reusable element, is affected with the non-attainable value(s) and kept in the list of reusable elements with non-attainable domains. In each product obtained from the solver, all the variables of the PLM are affected with a particular value of the corresponding domain. Thus, this algorithm takes advantage of that fact and records the answers given by the solver in order to avoid achieving useless requests testing the attainability of domain values that have already been obtained in precedent tests. The corresponding algorithm is as follows:

```
NonAttainableDomains(PLM M, Solver S) {
    S.charge(M);
    For (each variable V ∈ M) {
            For(each Di ∈ domain of V AND not in {PrecedentProducts}){
                    Product = S.getOneSolution("V = Di");
                    If (Product = "false") {
                            Write ("The domain " + Di + " of " + V + " is non-attainable");
                    }
                    Else {
                            PrecedentProducts += Product;
                    }
```

```
            }
        }
    }
```

For instance in our running example, if when asking for a product with *WidthResolution=800* we get a product
P1 = [UNIX=1, Cdrom=1, Usb=0, Net=0, UtilityProgram=1, FileMaintenance=1, Editing=1, UserInterface=1, Graphical=1, WidthResolution=800, HeightResolution=600, Shell=1, SH=1, TCSH=1, BASH=0, OnlineInfor=0, ProgrammingSupport=0].
This means both that *WidthResolution* can attain the value of 800, and that the rest of variables can attain the values assigned by the solver. Thus, for instance, it is not necessary to ask if the variable *UNIX* can attain the value of 1 or if *HeightResolution* can attain the value of 600.

d. **Dead-free reusable elements**: A reusable element is dead if it cannot appear in any product of the product line. This operation takes as input a PLM and a collection of reusable elements, and it returns the set of dead reusable elements, or false if there is none in the input list. Reusable elements can be dead because: (i) they are excluded by an element that appears in all products (also known as full-mandatory or core reusable elements, c.f. Von der Maßen & Lichter 2004; Benavides *et al.* 2005; Trinidad *et al.* 2008; Van den Broek & Galvão 2009); and (ii) they are wrongly constrained (e.g., an attribute of the feature is > 5 and < 3 at the same time, or a group cardinality is wrong defined). Elfaki et al. (2009) detect dead features by searching only for predefined cases, i.e. defined dead features in the domain-engineering process. Trinidad et al. (2006, 2008) detect dead features by finding all products and then searching for unused features. Van den Broek and Galvão (2009) detect dead features by transforming the FM into a generalized feature tree, and then searching the feature occurrences that cannot be true. To the better of our knowledge there is not details in literature about the way in which the other references have implemented this operation. Our approach evaluates each non-zero value of each reusable element's domain, and reuses each solution obtained from the solver in order to avoid useless computations. If a reusable element cannot attain any of its non-zero values, then the reusable element is dead. The reuse of the solutions previously obtained makes our dead artefacts detection technique scalable as showed below, by contrasts to the state of the art. The corresponding algorithm is presented as follows:

```
DeadReusableElements(PLM M, Solver S) {
    S.charge(M);
    DeadElementsList = all variables of M;
    For (each variable V ∈ DeadElementsList) {
            Product = S.getOneSolution("V > 0");
            If (Product = "false") {
                    Write ("The variable " + V + " is dead");
            }
            Else {
            Erase V and all the other non-zero variables obtained in Product from
DeadElementsList;
            }
    }
}
```

Our algorithm first creates a list of the reusable elements whose dead or non-dead condition is yet to be assessed. For example:
deadElements=[UNIX, Cdrom, Usb, Net, UtilityProgram, FileMaintenance, Editing, UserInterface, Graphical, WidthResolution, HeightResolution, Shell, SH, TCSH, BASH, OnlineInfor, ProgrammingSupport].
Then, our algorithm queries for a configuration based on reusable elements for which we still ignore if they are dead or not, and sieves the selected (and thus alive) elements from this list. For example, to know if *UtilityProgram* is dead or not, it is sufficient to query the solver for a product with *UtilityProgram=1*, which provides a product
P1 = [UNIX=1, Cdrom=1, Usb=0, Net=0, UtilityProgram=1, FileMaintenance=1, Editing=1, UserInterface=1, Graphical=1, WidthResolution=800, HeightResolution=600, Shell=1, SH=1, TCSH=1, BASH=0, OnlineInfor=0, ProgrammingSupport=0].
This means not only that the reusable element *UtilityProgram* is not dead, but also that the other elements with values different from 0 are not dead. Therefore these elements can be sieved from the list of dead elements. The test can be repeated until all elements are sieved. For example querying for products with *Usb =1*, the solver provides another product which means that this reusable element is not dead either. According to our algorithm, the variable *Usb*, and all the other non-zero variables, must be erased from the list of dead elements. At this point the list of dead elements is empty, which means that there are no dead elements in the product line model.
The purpose of the aforementioned list is to reduce the number of queries. For instance in this example, only two queries were necessary to evaluate all reusable elements. In contrast, 17 queries would have been required in the current state of the art algorithm. However, it is not possible to calculate in advance how many queries would be needed, or even, to guaranty that the minimal number of queries will be executed, as this depends on the configuration generated by the solver.

e. **False optional reusable elements**: a reusable element is false optional if it is included in all the products of the product line despite being declared optional (Von der Maßen & Lichter 2004; Benavides *et al.* 2005; Trinidad *et al.* 2008). This operation takes a PLM and a collection of reusable elements modeled as optional as input, and returns the set of false optional reusable elements, or *false* if no one exists. Trinidad et al. (2006, 2009) detect false optional features based on finding all products and then searching for common features among those which are not assigned as common. To verify if an optional reusable element is false optional, we query for a product that does not contain the reusable element at hand (setting the feature's value to 0). If there is no such product, then the reusable element we are evaluating is indeed false optional.

```
FalseOptionalReusableElements(PLM M, Solver S) {
    S.charge(M);
    FalseOptionalElementsList = all optional elements of M;
    For (each variable V ∈ FalseOptionalElementsList) {
            Product = S.getOneSolution("V = 0");
            If (Product = "false") {
                    Write (V + " is false optional");
            }
            Else {
                    Erase V and all the other variables with a Zero affectation into
Product, from DeadElementsList;
```

```
            }
      }
}
```

For example if we want to know whether the optional reusable component *Usb* is false optional of not, it is sufficient to request for a product without this component (*Support_usb=0*). The solver, in this case, returns the product *P1 = [UNIX=1, Cdrom=1, Usb=0, Net=0, UtilityProgram=1, FileMaintenance=1, Editing=1, UserInterface=1, Graphical=1, WidthResolution=800, HeightResolution=600, Shell=1, SH=1, TCSH=1, BASH=0, OnlineInfor=0, ProgrammingSupport=0]*, which means that this optional reusable element can take the value of 0, it is, be effectively optional.

2.3. **Redundancy-free:** according to the Oxford dictionary something redundant is something "able to be omitted without loss of meaning or function" (Oxford University 2008). Therefore, redundancy in a PLM is about the presence of reusable elements and variability constraints among them that can be omitted from the PLM without loss of semantic on the PLM. Redundant constraints in FMs are undesired because, although they do not alter the space of solutions, they may consume extra computational effort in derivation and analysis operations (Yan *et al.* 2009), and they are likely to generate inconsistencies when the PL evolves. For the sake of evolution, it is certainly better detect and correct these redundancies. In order to detect them in a PLM this chapter proposes an operation that takes a PLM and a constraint as input and returns *true* if removing the constraint does not change the space of solutions.

Three alternatives can be implemented to check if a relationship is redundant or not. The naïve algorithm consists in calculating all the products of the PLM with the constraint to check; then, remove the constraint; and calculate all the solutions of the new model. If both results are equal (i.e. exact the same products can be configured with and without the constraint), then the constraint is redundant. This approach is computationally very expensive as it requires (a) to compute all configurations twice and (b) to perform an intersection operation between two potentially very large sets (e.g. 10^{21} configurations for the Renault PLM according to Dauron & Astesana (2010)). Not only this algorithm is not scalable, it is typically unfeasible. The second algorithm, proposed by Yan *et al.* (2009) defines a redundant constraint of a PLM as a constraint in which a redundant reusable element takes part. This approach consists in calculating the redundant reusable elements on feature models – features disconnected from the FM – and then the redundant constraint in this approach are those in which the redundant features take part. Though it yields a solution, this algorithm is not sufficiently general: indeed, only these trivial cases of redundancy are considered. The approach proposed in this chapter is based on the fact that if a system is consistent, then the system plus a redundant constraint is consistent too. Therefore, negating the allegedly redundant relation implies contradicting the consistency of the system and thus rendering it inconsistent (Mazo *et al.* 2011a). This approach is more efficient, and thus more scalable, when applied on large models. Our algorithm is in two steps: first, it tries to obtain a solution with the set of constraints. Then, if a solution exists, we negate the constraint we want to check. In the case where no solution is found, the inspected constraint turns out to be redundant. This alternative to find redundant constraints can be formalized as follows:

```
If (at least 1 product can be configured from PLM M under a collection of constraints C
= {C1,...,Ci}) {
    Write (C |= M);
    Let take Cr ∈ C a constraint to be evaluated;
    If (C without Cr |= M AND C ∪ ¬Cr |≠ M) {
            Write (Cr is redundant);
    }
    Else{
            Write (Cr is not redundant);
    }
}
```

For example, to check if the constraint *UNIX* ≥ *UtilityProgram* (cf. Table 1) is redundant or not, it is sufficient to query the solver for a product. Then, if a product is found, the algorithm proceeds to replace the constraint by its negation (*UNIX* < *UtilityProgram*) and ask again for a product. If the solver does not give a solution (as is the case for our running example), one can infer that the constraint (*UNIX* ≥ *UtilityProgram*) is not redundant.

5. Multi-model verification

Multi-model modeling allows tackling various models and aspects of a system, in particular in the presence of stakeholders with multiple viewpoints (executives, developers, distributors, marketing, architects, testers, etc.; cf. Nuseibeh *et al.* 1994). For example, a UNIX product line can be composed of several models, each one developed by a different team or developing a particular view of the PL. Thus, while the team responsible of the kernel develops a model, the team responsible of the user interface develops another model. Motivated by the fact that (a) this practice is current in industry (Dhungana *et al.* 2010); (b) even if each individual model is consistent, once the models are integrated, they can easily be inconsistent; and (c) the lacks in current state of the art in multi-model PL verification, this chapter proposes a method to verify multi-model PLs. This method is composed of fourth steps: (i) the base models' semantic should be transformed into constraint programs; (ii) once these base models transformed into CP, they may be integrate using the integration strategies and rules appropriates for each language (cf. Mazo et al. 2011a for further details about integration of Dopler models, and Mazo *et al.* 2011d for further details about integration of constraint-based PLMs; and (iii) once the base models integrated, the collection of verification criteria, proposed in Section 4 for single models, can be applied on the integrated model in the same manner as for single models.

The application of these verification criteria over the Dopler model depicted in Figure 2 and the explanation regarding the minor variants are presented as follows:

1. **Non-void model**. This model is not a void because it allows configure at least one product; for instance *C1 = {USB, Editing, ProgrammingSupport, Shell}*
2. **Non-false model**. This model is not a false because it allows configure more than two products; for instance: *C2 = {Cdrom, Editing, OnlineInfo, Shell, Twm, KDE, Qt, GraphicalResolution = "800x600", Width = 800}* and *C3 = {USB, Editing}*.
3. **Non-attainable validity conditions' and domains' values.** This operation either (i) takes a collection of decisions as input and returns the decisions that cannot attain

one or more values of its validity condition; or (ii) takes a collection of assets as input and returns the assets that cannot attain one of the values of its domain. A non-attainable value of a validity condition or a domain is a value that can never be taken by a decision or an asset in a valid product. Non-attainable values are undesired because they give the user a wrong idea of the values that decisions and assets modeled in the product line model can take. In our example of Figure 2, the validity condition *Width ≥ 800 && Width ≤ 1366* determines a very large range of values that can take the variable Width, however this variable can really take three values: 800, 1024 and 1366 which means that values like 801, 802,..., 1023, 1025, ..., 1365 are not attainable values.

4. **Dead reusable elements.** In Dopler language, the reusable elements are Decisions and Assets. This operation takes a collection of decisions and assets as input and returns the set of dead decisions and assets (if some exist) or *false* otherwise. A decision is dead if it never becomes available for answering it. An asset is dead if it cannot appear in any of the products of the product line. The presence of dead decisions and assets in product line models indicates modeling errors and intended but unreachable options. A decision can become dead (i) if its visibility condition can never evaluate to true (e.g., if contradicting decisions are referenced in a condition); (ii) a decision value violates its own visibility condition (e.g., when setting the decision to true will in turn make the decision invisible); or (iii) its visibility condition is constrained in a wrong way (e.g., a decision value is > 5 && < 3 at the same time). An asset can become dead (i) if its inclusion depends on dead decisions, or (ii) if its inclusion condition is false and it is not included by other assets (due to *requires* dependencies to it). Dead variables in CP are variables than can never take a valid value (defined by the domain of the variable) in the solution space. Thus, our approach consists in evaluating each non-zero value of each variable's domain. If a variable cannot attain any of its non-zero values, the variable is considered dead. For instance, in the Dopler model of Figure 2, there are not dead decisions or assets.
5. **Redundancy-free**. In the asset model (cf. the right side of Figure 2) the asset *4dwn* requires *MwM,* which at the same time requires the asset *Motif,* therefore the dependency *4dwm* requires *Motif* is redundant according to the redundancy-free algorithm presented in Section 4.

It is worth noting that the domain-specific operation "false optional-free reusable elements" is not applicable in Dopler models due to the fact that this language does not have explicitly the concept of optional. Decisions and assets are optional in Dopler models according to the evaluation of the visibility conditions (in the case of decisions) and inter-assets dependencies in the case of assets

6. Validation

We performed a series of experiments to evaluate the verification approach proposed in this chapter. The goal was to measure the effectiveness or precision of the defect's detection, the computational scalability and the usability of the approach to verify different kinds of product line models. These measurements are presented in the next sections, grouped by the kind of product line models used to evaluate our approach.

6.1 Single-view models

We assessed the feasibility, precision and scalability of our approach with 46 models, out of which 44 were taken from the SPLOT repository (Mendonca *et al.* 2009b) and the other two models are the Vehicle movement control system (Salinesi *et al.* 2010b) and the Stago model (Salinesi et al. 2011). The sizes of the models are distributed as follows: 32 models of sizes from 9 to 49 features, 4 from 50 to 99, 5 from 100 to 999 and 6 from 1000 to 2000 features. The six largest feature models that we have were not considered in this experiment due to the fact that the solver used does not accept more that 5000 variables. Note that SPLOT models do not have attributes, on the contrary to our two industrial models. Therefore artificial attributes were introduced in a random way, in order to have models with 30%, 60% or 100% of their features with attributes. In order to do that, we created a simple tool[1] that translates models from SPLOT format to constraint programs, and we integrate next the artificial attributes. In order to test that the transformation respects the semantic of each feature model, we compared the results of our models without attributes with the results obtained with the tools SPLOT (Mendonca *et al.* 2009b) and FaMa (Trinidad *et al.* 2008b). In both comparisons we obtained the same results in all the shared functions: detection of void models, dead features, and false optional features. These results show that our transformation algorithm respects the semantic of initial models.

6.1.2 Precision of the detection

Not only must the transformation of FMs into CPs be correct but also the detection of defects. As aforementioned, we compared the results obtained with our tool VariaMos against these obtained with two other tools: SPLOT and FaMa. These comparisons were made over models without attributes due to the fact that original models taken from SPLOT, and also available for FaMa, do not have attributes. In these comparisons we find the same results, for the common verification functions on the three tools, but due to the fact that our own models contain attributes and group cardinalities <*m..n*>, for any *m* and *n* bellowing to non negative integer numbers, a manual inspection were necessary. A manual inspection on two samples of 28 and 56 features showed that our approach identify the 100% of the anomalies with 0% false positive.

6.1.3 Computational scalability

The execution time of the verification operations in our tool shows that the performance obtained with our approach is acceptable in realistic situations; because in the worst case, users can execute any verification operation less than 19 seconds for models up to 2000 features. Figure 4 shows the execution time of each one of the six verification operations in the 50 models. In Figure 4 each plot corresponds to a verification operation: Figure 4(1) corresponds to operation 1, Figure 4(2) corresponds to operation 2 and so on. Times in the Y axis are expressed in milliseconds (ms) and X axis corresponds to the number of features. It is worth noting that most of the results overlap the other ones; we avoid the use of a logarithmic scale in the X axis, to keep the real behaviour of the results.

[1] parserSPLOTmodelsToCP.rar available at: https://sites.google.com/site/raulmazo/

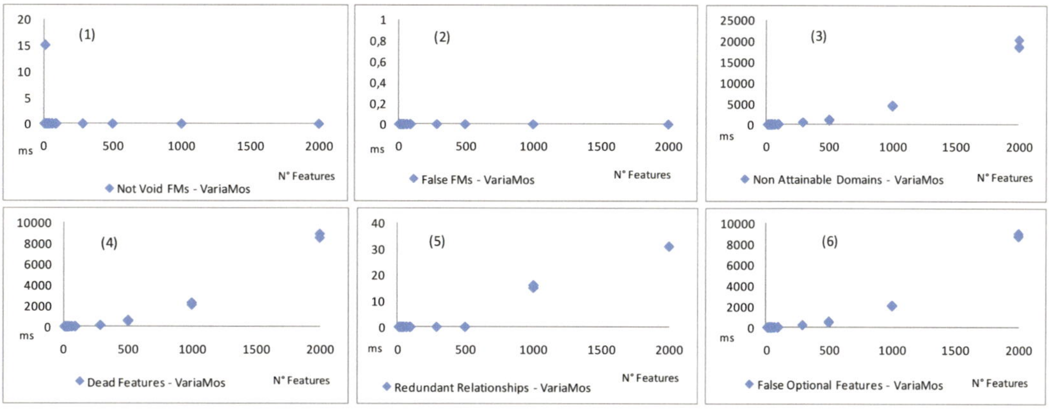

Fig. 4. Execution time of the six verification operations, per number of features

Let us now present the results in more detail. For the models with sizes between 9 and 100 features our approach verified all operations in less than 1 second on average. For the models with sizes between 101 and 500 features verified dead features and false optional features in 0,4 seconds, 1 second to calculate the non attainable domains and 0 milliseconds in the rest of verification operations. It is worth noting ant our solver does not provide time measures of microseconds (10^{-6} seconds); thus, 0 milliseconds (10^{-3} seconds) must be interpreted as less than 1 millisecond. In general, over the 46 FMs, the execution time to detect dead features, false optional features and non attainable domains is inferior than 8,68, 8,82 and 19,09 seconds respectively. For the rest of verification operations, the execution time is inferior to 0,02 seconds even for the largest models. Following the projection of our results, our approach is able to be used in larger FMs with a quadratic increase, in the worst of cases, of the time to execute any verification operation proposed in this paper. To finish, the verification operations like redundant relationships, false feature models and void feature models are executed in less than 0,03 seconds. According to the results of our experiment, we can conclude that our verification approach presented in this chapter is scalable to large FMs.

3.6 The case multi-view models

We also tested our verification approach with two Dopler variability models (Mazo *et al.* 2011a). In both models, we seeded 33 defects in the DOPLER model and 22 defects in the camera model. The defects cover different types of problems to show the feasibility of the verification approach. For instance, the decision *Wizard_height* cannot take the values 1200, 1050, 1024 and 768 and the asset *VAI_Configuration_DOPLER* cannot take the value 1 (is never included for any product), even if these values take part in the corresponding variables' domain. Furthermore, we measured the execution time of applying the approach for both models for the different verification operations as presented below.

Applying our verification approach to the DOPLER model has shown that the model is not void and can generate 23016416 products. However, we discovered 18 defects related with non-attainable domain values and 15 dead decisions and assets (these together are the 33 defects we have seeded before). By applying our verification approach on the digital camera model we obtained that the model is not void and can generate 442368 products. In this model, we discovered 11 defects related with non-attainable domain values as well as 11 dead decisions and assets (these together are the 22 defects we have seeded before). It is noteworthy that the same number of defects was identified in a manual verification of both models. The automated verification found all of the seeded defects in the DOPLER model and all of the seeded defects in the camera model.

Table 2 shows the number of defects found and the execution time (in milliseconds) corresponding to the verification operations on the models. No defects were found regarding the "Void model", "False model" and "Redundant relationships" operations and the execution time was less than 1 millisecond for each one of these operations in each model. The model transformations from Dopler models to constraint programs took about 1 second for each model.

		Void model	False model	Non-attainable domains	Dead Decisions and Assets	Redundant relationships
DOPLER 81 Variables	Defects	No	No	18	15	No
	Time	0	0	125	47	0
Camera 39 Variables	Defects	No	No	11	11	No
	Time	0	0	16	15	0

Table 2. Results of model verifications: Execution time (in milliseconds) and number of defects found with each verification operation.

In the same way as for the single-view models, the results obtained on multi-view models allow concluding that the verification approach presented in this chapter is scalable to medium Dopler models and give promising expectations on large Dopler models.

5. References

Batory D. (2005). Feature Models, Grammars, and Propositional Formulas. *In Proceedings of the International Software Product Line Conference (SPLC)*, pages 7-20. Rennes, France.

Benavides D. On the Automated Analysis of Software Product Lines Using Feature Models. A Framework for Developing Automated Tool Support. (2007). University of Seville, Spain, PhD Thesis.

Benavides, D., Segura, S., Trinidad, P., and Ruiz-Cortés, A. (2006). Using Java CSP solvers in the automated analyses of feature models. In Post-Proceedings of The Summer School on Generative and Transformational Techniques in Software Engineering (GTTSE). LNCS 4143.

Benavides, D., Segura, S., Ruiz-Cortés, A. (2010). Automated Analysis of Feature Models 20 Years Later: A Literature Review. Information Systems journal, Volume 35 , Issue 6, Elsevier, PP. 615-636

Benavides, D.; Trinidad, P. & Ruiz-Cortés, A. (2005). Automated Reasoning on Feature Models. *In Pastor, Ó., Falcão e Cunha, J. (eds.) CAiSE 2005*. LNCS, vol. 3520, pp. 491–503. Springer, Heidelberg.

Benavides, D.; Ruiz-Cortés, A.; Trinidad, P. (2005). Using constraint programming to reason on feature models. In The Seventeenth International Conference on Software Engineering and Knowledge Engineering, SEKE 2005, pages 677–682.

Bosch, J. (2000). *Design and Use of Software Architectures. Adopting and evolving a product-line approach.* Addison-Wesley.

Cabot, J. & Teniente, E. (2006). Incremental evaluation of ocl constraints. *In Dubois, E., Pohl, K. (eds.) CAiSE'06*. LNCS, vol. 4001, pp. 81–95. Springer, Heidelberg.

Clements, P. & Northrop, L. (2001). *Software Product Lines: Practices and Patterns.* Addison Wesley, Reading, MA, USA.

Czarnecki, K.; Pietroszek, K. (2006). Verifying Feature-Based Model Templates Against Well-Formedness OCL Constraints, 5th Int. Conference on Generative Programming and Component Engineering.

Czarnecki, K.; Helsen, S. & Eisenecker, U. W. (2005). Formalizing cardinality-based feature models and their specialization. *Software Process: Improvement and Practice*, 10(1), pp. 7-29.

Dauron, A. & Astesana, J-M. (2010). Spécification et configuration de la ligne de produits véhicule de Renault. *Journée Lignes de Produits.* Université Pantéon Sorbonne, France.

Dhungana, D.; Grünbacher, P. & Rabiser R. (2010). The DOPLER Meta-Tool for Decision-Oriented Variability Modeling: A Multiple Case Study. *Automated Software Engineering* (in press; doi: 10.1007/s10515-010-0076-6).

Dhungana, D.; Heymans, P. & Rabiser, R. (2010). A Formal Semantics for Decision-oriented Variability Modeling with DOPLER. *Proc. of the 4th International Workshop on Variability Modelling of Software-intensive Systems (VaMoS)*, Linz, Austria, ICB-Research Report No. 37, University of Duisburg Essen, 2010, pp. 29-35.

Dhungana, D., Rabiser, R. & Grünbacher, P. (2006). Coordinating Multi-Team Variability Modeling in Product Line Engineering. *In 2nd International Workshop on Supporting Knowledge Collaboration in Software Development (KCSD)*, Tokyo, Japan.

Diaz, D. & Codognet, P. (2001). Design and Implementation of the GNU Prolog System. *Journal of Functional and Logic Programming (JFLP)*, Vol. 2001, No. 6.

Djebbi, O.; Salinesi, C. & Fanmuy, G. (2007). Industry Survey of Product Lines Management Tools: Requirements, Qualities and Open Issues. *Proc. of the International Conference on Requirement Engineering (RE)*, IEEE Computer Society, New Delhi, India.

Djebbi, O. & Salinesi C. (2007). RED-PL, a Method for Deriving Product Requirements from a Product Line Requirements Model. *Proc. of the International Conference CAISE'07.* Norway.

Egyed, A. (2006). Instant consistency checking for UML. *In: International Conf. Software Engineering (ICSE'06)*, pp. 381–390. ACM Press, New York.

Elfaki, A.; Phon-Amnuaisuk, S. & Kuan Ho C. (2009). Using First Order Logic to Validate Feature Model. *Third International Workshop on Variability Modelling of Software-intensive Systems VaMoS.* ICB-Research Report No. 29, Universität Duisburg-Essen, pp. 169-172. Spain.

Finkelstein, A.C.W.; Gabbay, D.; Hunter, A.; Kramer, J. & Nuseibeh, B. (1994) Inconsistency handling in multiperspective specifications. *IEEE Transactions on Software Engineering*, pages 569–578.

Finkelstein, A.; Kramer, J.; Nuseibeh, B.; Finkelstein, L.; Goedicke, M. (1992). Viewpoints: A framework for integrating multiple perspectives in system development. International Journal of Software Engineering and Knowledge Engineering 2(1).

Griss, M.; Favaro, J. & d'Alessandro, M. (1998). Integrating feature modeling with the RSEB. *In Proceedings of the Fifth International Conference on Software Reuse*. Vancouver, BC, Canada.

Hemakumar, A. (2008). Finding Contradictions in Feature Models. Workshop on the Analysis of Software Product Lines (ASPL).

Howe, D. (2010). *The Free On-line Dictionary of Computing*, 01.06.2011, Available from http://foldoc.org

Janota, M.; Kiniry, J. (2007). Reasoning about Feature Models in Higher-Order Logic, in 11th Int. Software Product Line Conference (SPLC07).

Kang, K.; Cohen, S.; Hess, J.; Novak, W. & Peterson, S. (1990). Feature-Oriented Domain Analysis (FODA) Feasibility Study. *Technical Report CMU/SEI-90-TR-21, Software Engineering Institute*, Carnegie Mellon University, USA.

Kang, K.; Lee, J.; Donohoe, P. (2002). Feature-oriented product line engineering. Software, IEEE, 19(4).

Kim, C.H.P.; Batory, D.; Khurshid, S. (2011). Reducing Combinatorics in Testing Product Lines. Aspect Oriented Software Development (AOSD).

Lauenroth, K.; Metzger, A.; Pohl, K. (2010). Quality Assurance in the Presence of Variability. S. Nurcan et al. (eds.), Intentional Perspectives on Information Systems Engineering, Springer-Verlag, Berlin Heidelberg.

Lauenroth, K. & Pohl, K. (2007). Towards automated consistency checks of product line requirements specifications. *Proceedings of the twenty-second IEEE/ACM international conference on Automated software engineering ASE'07*, USA.

Liu, J.; Basu, S.; Lutz, R. R. (2011). Compositional model checking of software product lines using variation point obligations. Journal Automated Software Engineering, Volume 18 Issue 1.

Matthias, R.; Kai, B.; Detlef, S. & Ilka, P. (2002). Extending feature diagrams with UML multiplicities. *Proceedings of the Sixth Conference on Integrated Design and Process Technology*. Pasadena, CA.

Mazo, R.; Grünbacher, P.; Heider, W.; Rabiser, R.; Salinesi, C. & Diaz, D (2011). Using Constraint Programming to Verify DOPLER Variability Models. *In 5th International Workshop on Variability Modelling of Software-intensive Systems (VaMos'11)*, pp.97-103, ACM Press. Belgium.

Mazo, R.; Salinesi, C.; Diaz, D. & Lora-Michiels, A. (2011). Transforming Attribute and Clone-Enabled Feature Models into Constraint Programs Over Finite Domains. *6th International Conference on Evaluation of Novel Approaches to Software Engineering (ENASE)*, Springer Press, China.

Mazo, R.; Lopez-Herrejon, R.; Salinesi, C.; Diaz, D. & Egyed, A. (2011). A Constraint Programming Approach for Checking Conformance in Feature Models. *In 35th IEEE Annual International Computer Software and Applications Conference (COMPSAC'11)*, IEEE series, Germany.

Mazo, R.; Salinesi, C.; Djebbi, O.; Diaz, D. & Lora-Michiels, A. (2011). Constraints: the Heard of Domain and Application Engineering in the Product Lines Engineering Strategy. *International Journal of Information System Modeling and Design IJISMD* (accepted), to appear in November 2011.

Mazo, R.; Salinesi, C.; Diaz, D. (2011). Abstract Constraints: A General Framework for Solver-Independent Reasoning on Product Line Models. Accepted on INSIGHT - Journal of International Council on Systems Engineering (INCOSE), to be released the 15 October 2011.

Mendonça, M.; Wasowski, A. & Czarnecki, K. (2009). SAT–based analysis of feature models is easy. *In D. Muthig and J. D. McGregor, editors, SPLC, volume 446 of ACM International Conference Proceeding Series,* pp. 231-240. ACM.

Nuseibeh, B.; Kramer, J. & Finkelstein A. (1994)A framework for expressing the relationships between multiple views in requirements specification. *IEEE Trans. Software Eng.* 20(10) pp. 760–773.

Oxford University. 2008). *Concise Oxford English Dictionary*. Oxford University Press, UK.

Pohl, K.; Böckle, G.; van der Linden, F. (2005). Software Product Line Engineering - Foundations, Principles, and Techniques. Springer, Heidelberg.

Riebisch, M.; Bollert, K.; Streitferdt, D.; Philippow, I. (2002). Extending feature diagrams with UML multiplicities, in: Proceedings of the Sixth Conference on Integrated Design and Process Technology (IDPT2002), Pasadena, CA.

Salinesi, C.; Mazo, R. & Diaz, D. (2010). Criteria for the verification of feature models. *In Proceedings of the 28th INFORSID Conference,* pp. 293-308. France.

Salinesi, C.; Mazo, R.; Diaz, D. & Djebbi, O. (2010) Solving Integer Constraint in Reuse Based Requirements Engineering. *In 18th IEEE Int. Conference on Requirements Engineering (RE'10)* IEEE Computer Society pp. 243-251. Australia.

Salinesi, C. ; Mazo, R. ; Djebbi, O. ; Diaz, D. ; Lora-Michiels, A. (2011). Constraints: the Core of Product Line Engineering. Fifth IEEE International Conference on Research Challenges in Information Science (RCIS), IEEE Press, Guadeloupe-French West Indies, France.

Schobbens, P.Y.; Heymans, P.; Trigaux, J.C.; Bontemps Y. Generic semantics of feature diagrams, Journal of Computer Networks, Vol 51, Number 2 (2007).

Schulte, Ch.; Stuckey, P. J. (2008). Efficient constraint propagation engines. ACM Trans. Program. Lang. Syst., 31(1).

Segura, S. (2008). Automated Analysis of Feature Models using Atomic Sets. First Workshop on Analyses of Software Product Lines (ASPL'08), SPLC'08. Limerick, Ireland.

Stahl, T.; Völter, M. & Czarnecki, K. (2006). *Model-Driven Software Development: Technology, Engineering, Management.* Wiley editors, San Francisco.

Streitferdt, D.; Riebisch, M.; Philippow, I. (2003). Details of formalized relations in feature models using OCL. In Proceedings of 10th IEEE International Conference on Engineering of Computer–Based Systems (ECBS 2003), Huntsville, USA. IEEE Computer Society, pages 45–54.

Trinidad, P.; Benavides, D.; Durán, A.; Ruiz-Cortés, A. & Toro, M. (2008). Automated error analysis for the agilization of feature modeling. *Journal of Systems & Software,* 81(6) pp. 883-896, Elsevier.

Trinidad, P., Benavides, D., Ruiz-Cortés, A. (2006), A first step detecting inconsistencies in feature models. In CAiSE Short Paper Proceedings, Advanced Information Systems

Engineering, 18th International Conference, CAiSE 2006, Luxembourg, Luxembourg.

Van Hentenryck, P. (1989). Constraint Satisfaction in Logic Programming. The MIT Press.

Van den Broek, P. & Galvão, I. (2009). Analysis of Feature Models using Generalised Feature Trees. *Third International Workshop on Variability Modelling of Software-intensive Systems VaMoS*. ICB-Research Report No. 29, Universität Duisburg-Essen, pp. 169-172. Spain.

Van der Storm, T. (2007). Generic Feature-Based Composition. In: M. Lumpe and W. Vandeperren, editors, Proceedings of the Workshop on Software Composition (SC'07), volume 4829 of LNCS, pp. 66-80, Springer.

Von der Maßen, T. ; Lichter, H. (2003). RequiLine: A requirements engineering tool for software product lines, Proceedings of International Workshop on Product Family Engineering PFE-5, Springer LNCS 3014, Siena, Italy.

Von der Maßen, T. & Lichter, H. (2004). Deficiencies in feature models. *In Tomi Mannisto and Jan Bosch, editors, Workshop on Software Variability Management for Product Derivation - Towards Tool Support.*

White, J.; Doughtery, B.; Schmidt, D. (2009). Selecting highly optimal architectural feature sets with filtered cartesian flattening. Journal of Systems and Software, 82(8):1268–1284.

Yan, H.; Zhang, W.; Zhao, H. & Mei, H. (2009). An optimization strategy to feature models' verification by eliminating verification-irrelevant features and constraints. *In the proceedings of the International Conference on Software Reuse (ICSR)*, pp. 65–75.

Zhang, W.; Zhao, H.; Mei, H. (2004) A Propositional Logic-Based Method for Verification of Feature Models. In: Proceedings of 6th International Conference on Formal Engineering Methods, pp. 115–130.